Gerald E. Cumby

The
Bridge
Builder

ISBN: 1460992202
ISBN-13: 9781460992203

With his hands, his character, and his principles, my dad built bridges. He was the benchmark or paradigm of fatherhood and the ambassador of goodwill for those who needed help in the storms of life.

Author

Gerald Cumby is retired from General Dynamics/Lockheed Martin, Aeronautics Division. His career at Lockheed Martin included 38 years in management. He taught and coached in the Texas Public Schools in his early years and has fulfilled his desire for teaching as he has taught 13 years of Certified Manager courses while at Lockheed Martin and Sunday School/Bible Study classes since he was 15 years old. He is a Certified Professional Manager (CPM) and has his Bachelor of Science in Education Degree from McMurry University and his Masters from Tyndale Seminary in Biblical Studies. His desire for coaching has been fulfilled as a baseball/softball umpire and basketball referee for over 25 years. He has umpired and/or refereed over 5,000 games before his retirement.

He and his wife, Sherry, live in Burleson, Texas. They have been blessed to be married for 50 years. His married children, Tami Barber and Melanie Dickson, have also blessed the family with two children of their own. They have been married to their sweethearts for 26 and 28 years respectively.

Gerald has had several articles published in Automotive Fleet, Business Fleet, and other Automotive/Material Handling magazines over the years. His passion is to see people come to the saving knowledge of Jesus and works in several organizations that emphasize evangelism. Child Evangelism Fellowship (CEF) and the Good News Programs (children's after-school program in the public schools) around the world have been part of his life for the last several years.

Gerald Cumby, Author of The Bridge Builder

Picture: Bridge on Tara Shalom, Gates of Peace, built by the author after retiring: it connects the "Little Green Acre" God gave Gerald and Sherry in 1993 with Tami and Doug's place.

"Finally, brothers, whatever is true, whatever is noble, whatever is right, whatever is pure, whatever is lovely, whatever is admirable—if anything is excellent or praiseworthy—think about such things"
(Philippians 4:8).

Dedication:

This book is dedicated to the most important living person in my life. My wife, Sherry Yancey Cumby, has been my partner in life for over 50 years. She has been an inspiration for living, an encouraging and uplifting companion as we work and play together, and a gentle and loving sweetheart, in which I would give my life if necessary. She has encouraged me to write down my experiences of "growing up" and mission trips with my dad and mom as they made the decisions that affected our family and many others struggling with the problems life dealt them.

Sherry gave me important mentoring as she helped me understand how important it is to journal and pass on valuable information to our children and grandchildren. She would hear the stories about my dad and mom and would reply on many occasions, "You need to write that down as a treasure for the family after we are gone."

Sherry knew my dad only through the stories that I and others in my family related to her. However, she first heard about him at the age of 11 when the story of my dad's death was on the front page of the local paper. When that article appeared in the paper, Sherry's mother read the news report aloud at the breakfast table and Mac, Sherry's stepfather, who worked for my dad at one time, spoke of what a fine man Jay Cumby was and described him as a man he truly enjoyed as a boss.

The Bridge Builder is mainly about my father and mother. However, the lady that I am dedicating this book is as much of a Bridge Builder as any person I know. She is truly the "Princess" in which I address her every morning. I don't deserve the title, but she feels I am her "Prince in shining armor."

One of these days, the prince and the princess will bow before the King. It will be an honor to see Him face to face and tell Him how much we love Him....together!

Hymn/Song Texts

At the end of each chapter of *The Bridge Builder*, there is a hymn or song text with no music (notes)—just words. As much as I like to sing the hymns of our faith, I love the words that touch our hearts much more than the sound of music that touches our senses.

The words of these great hymns cling to the heart and melt our inhibitions to the point of desiring to praise the Lord. That's where the praise begins! If you want to "make a joyful noise unto the Lord" after reading the words, that would be the normal reaction to the "sinner who has come home."

I hope that you, the reader, take the opportunity to read the words that make up our great hymns of yesteryear that tie in with the chapters of *the Bridge Builder*. The words of the hymns are sermons in themselves.

We react to what we hear and remember. We react to what we know to be the truth. Although many of the words of the hymns are not quotes of Scripture, they do, however, reach into the heart of the person that has been changed by the Scriptures and the One in whom the Scriptures reveal as "the Truth" and gives him/her a sense of compatibility and close relationship with the Almighty.

Table of Contents

❧❧

The Bridge Builder

By Will Allen Dromgoole

The Bridge Builder is often reprinted and remains quite popular. It continues to be quoted frequently, usually in a religious context or in writings stressing a moral lesson. It is also a favorite of motivational speakers.

Many fraternities use *The Bridge Builder* to promote the idea of building links for the future and passing the torch along to the next generation.

It was possibly first published in 1900 in the now rare book *A Builder.*

This poem is a prologue to the experiences addressed in this book in which the reader will, hopefully, find quite intriguing and enlightening. Although the experiences recalled in this writing are from the viewpoint of a young and inquisitive red-blooded American boy born a few years prior to the Baby Boomer Generation, they do reflect the same reasoning as to one feeling a need to leave a moral legacy and acceptable family values for the next generation. This poem does not have a surprise ending; only the flare for the charm and appeal of an inquisitive audience that wants the whole story, not just the summarized version.

The Bridge Builder

By Will Allen Dromgoole

An old man, going a lone highway,
Came, at the evening, cold and gray,
To a chasm, vast, and deep, and wide,
Through which was flowing a sullen tide.

The old man crossed in the twilight dim
The sullen stream had no fear for him;
But he turned, when safe on the other side,
And built a bridge to span the tide.

"Old man," said a fellow pilgrim, near,
"You are wasting strength with building here;
Your journey will end with the ending day;
You never again will pass this way;

You've crossed the chasm, deep and wide,

Why build you this bridge at the evening tide?"
The builder lifted his old gray head:
"Good friend, in the path I have come," he said,
"There followeth after me today,
A youth, whose feet must pass this way.

This chasm, that has been naught to me,
To that fair-haired youth may a pitfall be.
He, too, must cross in the twilight dim;
Good friend, I am building this bridge for him."

Foreword:

The Bridge Builder

Bridges and bridge builders are important. We need and rely on bridges for accessibility to life's necessities while the skills of the bridge builders ensure the safety of those bridges for our family and friends as they travel over our highways to life's appointments. The reality is that one day each of us will have an appointment to cross the bridge to eternity and we will want to personally know who was the builder and where does it go.

My dad, Earl Bailey, after dropping out of school at the age of fourteen, went to work for a firm building a bridge near his home in West Texas. After years of preparation he organized his own company and sub-contracted his first job in building the bridges and culverts on U.S. Highway 84 starting fifteen miles south of Abilene. That project was the beginning of Bailey Bridge Company and a long relationship with the Cumby family. One of the best decisions my dad made was the hiring as his lead foreman, Jay Cumby, a true West Texan.

My bridge building also began as a fourteen year old. I was son of the owner and during school worked on Saturdays with the bridge building crew. In the summer, I would then work an average of about 55 hours per week gaining skills and knowledge of bridge building.

I was under Jay's supervision. I can still hear him laugh and jokingly tell all the other workers, "You know, with Bob working here, he'll get the blame if anything goes wrong."

No one worked harder than Jay Cumby. The tasks he expected his crew to do he was there beside them performing the same or similar task. His every move seemed to be the correct one. Jay knew the advantage of being a positive and true leader of men. I remember an incident when one 'hot headed' worker took offense at his leadership and challenged him to a fight. Jay told him, "If you want to fight I'm ready….and you may whip me. But when we get through, I want you working with me because you are a good worker." There was no fight and Jay and the hotheaded workman became great friends.

Over the years Jay Cumby's sons were added as 'Bridge Builders' to our company. First there was Joe, then Doyle who also became a leader, and later Gerald and Randy. All these men were quality; not only because of a wonderful and loving dad, but because they were also blessed with a precious, hard working mother that remained a stable force in their lives.

I well remember Jay's tragic death years later. For years the loss of our 'Bridge Builder Leader' affected us all. We don't understand all the reasons why, but we know that something considered good can come from tragedy when God is in control.

In the '70's my dad semi-retired and I took over the management of Bailey Bridge Company. My first bid was a co-bid with a Dallas contractor to construct one of the largest intersections in Texas - I-20 and US 67 in southwest Dallas. The 420-acre project included 22 major structures including one massive and towering overpass spanning 1,400 feet and rising 72 feet above the ground. This was a much larger project than anything we had ever done.

I chose Jay Cumby's oldest son, Joe, as Superintendent for that major project. Doyle was a lead foreman and worked with us for years. Two of the younger brothers, Gerald and Randy, worked part-time during the summer while they were in high school and college. Tony was too young to get in on the action, but if he had been old enough I'm sure that he would have worked for us also.

Today there are times we need bridges in our lives to help us 'cross over'. God knew this from the beginning and offered His Son as the Bridge to life everlasting. Let me very loosely paraphrase verses from the fourteenth chapter of John.

"Jesus told his disciples 'don't worry about how you get from here to there. I am the bridge that will take you across. Trust me for My Father chose me as the bridge to get you to a special place on the other side. I am going over there soon to be sure that it is ready for you. When it's your time to cross, I will come back and lead you across my bridge so we can be on the other side together. Those of you who think there are other crossings need to know this truth… "I am the only bridge that takes you to the Father. No one can get to Him unless you cross with me on my bridge."

The Cumby men were the kind of leaders that every owner desires on his dream-team. I was blessed because years ago my dad chose Jay Cumby and his sons, and together we all became Bridge Builders. Any person who has driven across Texas has surely crossed bridges that one member of their family helped build. The Cumby name will always remain a part of bridge building in Texas.

Bob Bailey, Retired Highway Bridge Contractor,
Bailey Bridge Company

My Story...

The Bridge Builder

Preface:

"By the grace God has given me, I laid a foundation as an expert builder, and someone else is building on it. But each one should be careful how he builds" (1 Corinthians 3:10).

There is no definition for "bridge builder" according to Webster. I have a definition but Webster does not. The World Book Dictionary definition does not define "bridge builder;" but does define "bridgeman" as "a person whose work is in building bridges." My definition goes much deeper. A bridge builder is a "person that builds bridges (1) over obstacles in order to safely attain passage from one side of the obstacle to the other, (2) over treacherous and/or crooked and unsure paths in the lives of people so they might make it safely to the other side."

My father fits the definition in both areas...and could truly be called "the Bridge Builder" for my family as well as many others. Hopefully, with my story the reader of this book will also be encouraged, enlightened, and challenged to become a better person, a better parent, a better son or daughter where "bridge-building" will be a trait carried on from generation to generation.

My dad was a bridge builder, indeed. Constructively speaking, he built bridges across Texas - mainly in the Western and upper Northern plains of this great state. If you have ever driven across Texas on any of the major interstates or state highways, you have crossed a bridge on which my dad built. Some of these bridges have been replaced, but only because the major roads have been rerouted or widened to accommodate the increased flow of traffic in the last few decades. It is estimated that my dad built a minimum of 350 bridges or culverts throughout Texas. Of course, listening to him tell it, it would not be that "he" built them; but that he was only one member of a team that accomplished this great work in which truckers with their products and families going to visit parents and friends would have a safe and secure means of crossing creeks and rivers, valleys and streams, mountains and hills, railroad over-passes, and major cross-roads. Many of these major construction projects are still crossed after 64 years.

Just as anything of this world made of man-made materials deteriorates, the bridges constructed with calloused hands and hard work will also deteriorate with time. I believe, however, the bridges that my father helped me and others build in our attitudes, minds and memories will not deteriorate over the generations because we will make sure that his legacy of hard-work, steadfast principles, and godly precepts will be passed on to our children and to our children's children.

We have heard from many preachers and great statesman of our time the old adage: "behind every good man there is a good woman cheering him on." But I can tell you that that statement is <u>not</u> exactly true. It should read: "**At the side** of every good man there is truly a good woman cheering and encouraging him to meet responsibilities, helping him keep schedules and be successful in his endeavors."

My mother never built a bridge on which vehicles traveled over or under, but she did build bridges for boys and girls, young men, and women helping them to reach new heights with better attitudes and more disciplined lives due to her godly character and wise counsel.

What a joy to have been under my mom and dad's influence as a young boy growing up! For as troubled waters run through our minds and hearts, our God provides the bridges to help us cross to pastures green and fields that exhibit peace and contentment. Isn't it wonderful to know that there are promises a plenty with the assurance from God's Word that they will be fulfilled for those who commit themselves to the Lord? God's Word tells the faithful and trusted to "*Commit to the Lord whatever you do, and your plans will succeed*" (Proverbs 16:3).

Chapter 1

Building Blocks

"By wisdom a house is built, and through understanding it is established; through knowledge its rooms are filled with rare and beautiful treasures" (Proverbs 24:3-4).

At thirteen years old, a young man is ready to give the world a try at most anything. Usually at this age, however, a young man doesn't understand the consequences that might be in the future for the decisions he has made as he begins to jump into a world that seems so eager to accept his challenges. In my case, I was ready to make my mark as an athlete and as a business entrepreneur (lemon-aid stands, selling coke bottles at the nearest store, and taking orders for magazines from my industrious neighbors). I had no worries at all as I dropped off to sleep at night right after my mom said "good-night" and the most important part, that of telling me she loved me. If Dad was home, he would say the same thing mom did and all was right and polite in my little world.

Trying to make the largest kite in the world, the most treasured sling shot or bow and arrow from the nearest mesquite tree, or finding the straightest wooden tree limb that I could use to pole-vault over the 8' back fence were the things I thought about before going to bed at night. I was so mature for my age, I didn't have time to think about girls or the ugly world that was ready to soak up my over-zealous energy. To be truthful, my maturity level was maybe a little more than the squirrels that eagerly crossed the street without noticing the fast-paced vehicles that crossed the same path.

On this day in April 1955, I stood at the end of the pole-vault runway at Fair Park Stadium in Abilene, Texas, ready to take my 2nd vault trying to win a blue ribbon in the track event I loved so much. I had bandages on both hands from the chinning event the previous day. Blisters had turned into burning sores; but, I couldn't let that bother me for I was concentrating on getting over that bar that was standing between me getting a 2nd place or a 1st place ribbon.

Dad had placed those bandages on my hands the previous night. As he was pouring a soothing anesthetic on my wounds, he had tears in his eyes. As the tears ran down his face, he made the statement to me, "Why in the world, son, would you injure yourself so bad just to get a ribbon that probably cost less than a dollar." Although the palms of my hands were calloused due to the practice sessions the previous days and weeks in getting ready for the big event, the actual event brought a desire to do everything in my power to win. In other words, the win was worth it all to me, even if it did cause me pain. As to the answer to my dad's question I then stated, "For the same reason you work so hard, Dad; for the same reason you give your all to be the best."

Ready to vault, I now picked up the small metal pole-vaulting pole and was in the process of rocking back to go full force toward the pole vault pit and the bar that was raised to the highest level that I had ever tried when my coach stopped me in my tracks to tell me to go with him immediately. His countenance was not one that I had ever seen before. He was stern and seemed to have tears in his eyes. I hesitated and stated to the coach, "But Coach, if I go now I will be scratched from the event. I have to vault or I will not be given a chance to win." The coach said, "Drop the pole and come with me. You have a family member waiting to speak with you."

I remember that day like it was yesterday. I know the color of the track shorts I was wearing and the new black and white over-the-ankle tennis shoes my dad had bought me the previous weekend. I can picture the coach running ahead of me toward the south end of the field toward the field house where my sister-in-law was waiting for me. She had some life-changing words to say to me and my world was penetrated to the core as those six words were stated in about 5 seconds.

There are some famous 6-word statements that have been said that mean something to more people than this 13 year-old boy. Henry Ford stated, "Don't find fault. Find a remedy." That made an impact on the automobile industry as a whole. In the movie, *Forest Gump*, Forest stated, "Life's like a box of chocolates." Well, it isn't; but life is a mixture of ups and downs that continually direct and intertwine and connect to our thoughts and actions for days, weeks, and even years to come.

Winston Churchill said, "Broadly speaking, the short words are the best, and the old words best of all." Those are not six words, but are certainly in line with what I had to deal with as I have mulled over and wept over the six words that were said as I approached my sister-in-law at the track meet that fateful day. Those 6 words in 5 seconds had the impact of a freight train on my life. You will see what I mean as my story moves on in this writing.

At 13 and this stage of life, my world consisted of family meals, school, sports, and waiting for my dad to come home. In his coming home, we knew what the normal schedule was; that being of him taking a bath, sitting down at the dinner table with his wife and kids, and telling stories of the day's work with the gang of bridge builders in which he was in charge. When I went to sleep at night, I had no fear of my dad's wrath against me, my mother, or my five siblings. I never worried about my parents' divorcing or separating. There was love, comfort, a warm meal waiting for us every morning by a mom that loved her family, and sheer peace of knowing that anything and everything that happened to me, my parents were at my side.

If the things that happened to me were my fault, I would have to explain with no half-truths, lies or manipulation. If discipline were in order, I would certainly get it. Usually from my dad, but Mom knew that she had his permission to deal with the problems as she saw fit. And….we boys knew it, too. We knew that if she didn't handle it, he would! What Mom said was "gospel." What she thought of a situation was very important. It was for my dad....and "it better be for us," as he would say.

We were not wealthy or considered to be "upper class" in any way. In fact, we were reluctantly called middle class. Let's just say, we were the average American family, making a living from week-to-week; going about our business with no major cares or worries about where our next meal was coming from. We just loved our family times together....and that family time was usually spent around the dinner table. Sometime the conversations would go from 7 p.m. to 9 p.m....just sitting, nibbling on what was left on the table, and drinking iced tea until we were ready to go to bed. Every one had their turn in conversation, but Mom was just charmed and fascinated with Dad's stories of the men at work. Mom knew every one of the workers; not personally, but through my dad's stories. She could tell you the names of the wives and children of every one of Dad's bridge gang. She cried with my dad when one of the workers would lose one of their family members or one would be in the hospital due to illness or injury. She supported my dad in every thing he did. My dad was king in our home....and, no doubt, my mom was queen in Dad's heart. She knew it....and we knew it.

My dad and mom married at a very early age. They grew up together living in the same small community (Jim Ned area) and went to the same little country school from the start of their education.

One teacher taught all the grades in the one-room schoolhouse. To help the teacher, the older kids helped the younger kids with their Math, English, and the other learning areas of life (basically the 3 Rs were taught). The teacher handled all discipline problems (she was the only employee of the school; thus, the teacher, principal, and janitor) and every child knew that what the teacher said was very important and, most of the time, unquestionable.

There were times when the children would be given the opportunity to ask questions. The whole school, all ages from the 1st through the 10th grade listened to the students ask questions and heard the answer by the teacher (only 10 years of school were available and required for a diploma). The older children helped with the younger ones with all of their lessons and encouraged them to do their best every day.

Boys were expected to do their chores in the morning before they left for school. Girls would help their moms cook biscuits and gravy along with some homemade sausage and bacon. This was the natural and expected routine for most of the families throughout the community. Children did not know a different way of life (praise God). They just knew from the beginning of learning that helping each other, supporting and obeying their parents as well as others in authority, were not options. It was expected; it was unquestionable; it was the right thing to do and, if you didn't, you were realistically "biting the hand that fed you."

The Bible was read and was not thought of as an archaic book. It was the Book of all books. All other books and knowledge gained were based on "the Book." Wow, what a revelation! What a wise and progressive thought! To think that there might have been any other Book of Wisdom was not in anyone else's mind and thoughts.

And, you know, maybe we are on to something here. Could it be...that instead of twisting the minds of children with worldly and ungodly materials as reading requirements to "enlighten" them, that in going back to our roots of Biblical and God provided wisdom for living...might be to our better good? Are algebra, solid geometry, and chemistry more important than home economics for girls and basic auto mechanics or basic home repair for boys? Or, more important than that, is it more advantageous to gain God's wisdom or man's storehouse of knowledge?

You know, I am all for education. I have my college degree with a Masters. I have helped in sending both my children to college with the understanding that they would work during their time at college. I want the reader to know that this was not a forced issue on my daughters (working while going to college). They were working when they were in high school so it wasn't an issue that we really had to stress.

My wife, Sherry, the 12th of 13 children, has her teaching degree and has retired as a public school teacher in the State of Texas. We love to learn and at the age of 70 and 68 respectively we are still enjoying the wealth of learning. However, there has been more education taught by our parents that helped us in life than any book or college professor could ever possibly achieve.

Take it from me, life is short and times will get tough; however, your training and your will to live life to the fullest is the most important thing you can do. The only way anyone can live life to the fullest and come to the end of it and say, "I have fought the good fight, I have finished the race, I have kept the faith" is to be a servant of Jesus Christ. Placing my faith and trust in the only God and His Son has been the ticket to the better life. Heaven is real and because of God's promise to His children (those that know Him through Jesus), "there is in store for me the crown of righteousness, which the Lord, the righteous Judge, will award to me on that day—and not only to me, but also to all who have longed for his appearing," 2 Timothy 4:7-8.

Dad and Mom never took algebra, chemistry, or advanced English courses. However, without going past the 10th grade in a one-room schoolhouse, they could do more than many college gurus do after 6 years and $100,000 paid in college and university tuitions.

Dad could do math in his head without using a pencil, calculator, or slide rule. As a bridge construction superintendent, he had to be able to read the plans and perform to those plans.

One of Dad's co-workers told the following story. Federal and State inspectors were on my dad's jobs most of the time. It was time for a large concrete pour and the inspector asked Dad did he want him (the inspector, a construction engineer) to figure how much concrete to order. Dad told him that he already knew how much concrete to order and he had already told the concrete company to send out 96 cubic yards of pre-mixed concrete (about 12 truck loads). Taking the time to measure the exact dimensions of the area of the bridge in which the concrete was to be unloaded and graded, the inspector went into his office to calculate with a slide rule and calculator how much concrete it would take. The inspector came back about 45 minutes later to tell Dad that 96 yards was close, but he really needed 99 yards to assure that there was enough. He asked my dad how he came up with the figure and dad told him he measured the area just like the inspector did and that he calculated in his head how much concrete to deliver. The inspector was surprised and puzzled when the pour was made and completed using 95½ yards of concrete. My dad, to me, was not only Superman in work clothes, but he was Mr. Wise man, Incorporated.

Mom could write letters with proper grammar, punctuation, and spelling. She could balance her checkbook and could count out change (more than I can say for many students working in restaurants today). She knew just exactly how much money she had in the bank and, as far as I know, never did over-draw her account (more than I can say for some of our congressman today). She never learned how to drive a car, but she could read a recipe and make the best biscuits and gravy in the world. I loved her "drop biscuits" and "round potato sandwiches." Her chocolate pies were the best in the country (she did not use a recipe or measuring spoons/cups). My dad would eat her cooking, pat her on the back side and say, "Honey, that is better than Betty Crocker's cooking!" Mom would just kiss his cheek and say, "All for you, dear, all for you!" The kids would listen, learn, and go to bed knowing that every thing is all right in this little world of ours.

Incidentally, all of us kids wanted to know who Betty Crocker was but was afraid to ask. We finally found out she must be a pretty important lady because she had her name on a lot of boxes in the grocery store.

"Children, obey your parents, for this is right" (Ephesians 6:1).

"Children's children are a crown to the aged, <u>and parents are the pride of their children</u>" (Proverbs 17:6)

Hymn of a National call for Committed Fathers:

"God of our fathers, whose almighty hand leads forth
    in beauty, all the starry band.
Of shining worlds in splendor thru the skies, our grate-
    ful songs before Thy throne arise.
Thy love divine hath led us in the past, in this free land
    by Thee our lot is cast;
Be Thou our Ruler, Guardian, Guide, and Stay; Thy
    Word our law, Thy paths our chosen way.
Refresh Thy people on their toilsome way, lead us from
    night to never ending day;
Fill all our lives with love and grace divine, and glory,
    laud, and praise be forever Thine."

National Hymn, "God of Our Fathers",
Text by Daniel C. Roberts.

❦

Chapter 2

Building Assets

"A generous man will prosper; he who refreshes others will himself be refreshed" (Proverbs 11:25).

If there was ever a hero in my life, my dad was it. He still is...in my heart...and memory. There was no personal pride in my dad's heart; only pride in his family and what was accomplished by his team of workers, in whom, he claimed were "the best."

My dad grew up on a farm around Lawn, Texas. Lawn is a "big" city (population around 300) in Central Texas about 20 miles South of Abilene, near Tuscola (population 700). Tuscola, Texas was where Colt McCoy (University of Texas quarterback and now a professional quarterback in the NFL) went to high school (I know that will get your attention). Dad farmed and picked cotton for a living until he was around 34-35 years old. By this time, he had 4 children, 3 boys and one daughter; me being the youngest. I was only two or three years old at that time. Dad's hands were calloused and his skin on his face was "crisp from the sun" (according to Mom) and he found that life might be a little better if he would take his hands off of the plow and try working for a living as an employee...not the self-employed farmer.

Dad gained good common sense as a member of a farm family. His dad was a well-respected farmer who was a deacon in the community Methodist Church (about 40 members) and his mother was a stay-at-home mom that kept the house and home clean (really clean.... no dirt in the house and no filthy talk). My mother's father was the Baptist preacher across the street from the Methodist Church (about 40 members). Her mom played the piano in the church and prayed for the family....a lot.

Dad and Mom grew up together, going to the same little country school in the Jim Ned community just east of Lawn. They were married when mom was 16 and dad was 17. They didn't know anything other than work and work some more. They had their first child 6 years (noticed I said years) after they married. Joe was a big baby....12 lbs. and a few ounces. Yes, I know, "ouch." The joke around the house that dad would tell was that Joe was walking before my mom. Dad had told us that he nearly lost Mother when she was giving birth to Joe. Even so, Mom did not let that bother her. She had another child (a daughter) two years later. Referring back to the "common sense" I said my dad had, one might question that statement. You might be saying, "Why would anyone think he had common sense while fathering child after child"....six in all; me being #4. In those days, pregnancy and child bearing were not just commonplace....but, "the sensible thing" to do for the married couple who loved each other.

Birth control was not practiced. Work and more work gave little time to find time to court and charm each other. If the wife became pregnant, this was all in the plan of a Holy God. Since it was common and biblical for married couples to "multiply and replenish the earth," Dad and Mom did their duty and God blessed them for it.

This was just the way it was back then. In the world today, one might look at it and say, "This was no way to raise a child." However, for my dad and mom, they did it right. He used common sense as a dad making decisions that would affect his family…and mom used her "female instincts" to know what was right and how to do things that would be progressive and have a positive impact on our family.

And so…. my story is one that is typical and normal of the era back in the early 40's and 50's. Dad loved Mom, Mom loved Dad, both parents loved their children….and the children respected and loved their parents. What has happened to cause such a change in the typical American family? What have we done in our generation to have caused such disrespect for God, parents, country and others? Is there a factor that a nation, a people, a family can pinpoint as to where the problem is? I think there is…and we will try to address those areas of concern with some thoughts and ideas as my story moves along in this writing.

The stories and tales that you will hear as you read this book are those stories that are told as I either experienced first hand or those that were told to me. Minds are different and sometimes confusing. What one person sees and hears might be taken from a different perspective than what another experienced and heard. Again, minds center in on an experience and we believe it happened just the way we remember it....or want to remember it. This is not to say that it did not happen this way. It is only to say that how my siblings or friends remember experiences at home might be different than mine. I can only say, "To God be the glory when lives and hearts are touched by others as they walk, talk, and carry on the family traditions that help us through our struggles in life."

As we meet life's struggles head-on, we can either praise God for helping us through them or blame Him for not giving us what <u>we</u> "think best." God, help us to choose to let you mold us into Your character, not ours.

Hymn of a Happy Home:

"Happy the home when God is there and love fills
 everyone,
When with united work and prayer the Master's will is
 done.
Happy the home where God's strong love is starting to
 appear,
Where all the children hear His fame and parents hold
 Him dear.
Happy the home where prayer is heard and praise is
 everywhere,
Where parents love the sacred Word and its true wis-
 dom share.
Lord, let us in our homes agree this blessed peace to
 gain;
Unite our hearts in love to Thee, and love to all will
 reign."

Words from the song, "Happy the Home When God is There"
Text by Henry Ware, Jr.; altered by Bryan Jeffery Leech.

Chapter 3

Building Foundations

Job 19:4 states, "If it is true that I have gone astray, my error remains my concern alone."

What a true and strong statement (the Scripture above) for personal accountability of one's own sin. However, only in the context of the message and the predicament Job was referring is this statement applicable. What we know...and the Lord knows to be true, is that our sins and errors <u>do not just affect ourselves....our sins affect others</u>. Yes, we will give an account for our wickedness, our actions, and our misdeeds. However, I think that the most alarming reality of standing before our God is the fact that we have hurt others in the process of failing ourselves and our Lord.

Sometime our failures reap failures and sometime our wickedness begets wickedness. To see the frailties, failures and destructive tendencies in our lives and what it caused for others will be the most horrifying, most devastating time of our court hearing before God. We will have to cry, "We deserve to be cast out of heaven.... we don't deserve to be in the same place with those that did not cause stress, duress, and turmoil in the lives of others." I think when we see that our mistakes, our temper tantrums, our acts of rage against others caused such a horrific outcome in the lives of others, we will bow our head and be the judge of our own self....and declare ourselves "Guilty, Oh Lord, guilty as charged."

To place the above paragraph in this part of our story would, at first, seem out of place. However, you have to understand why it is here. My dad would be the first to tell you that he was not the father that took his family to church and all was well with the world. Although he had been raised in church, he did not think it was critical for our family to have the fellowship with other Christians that would be found in the local church body. He cherished his time with his family and I cherished my time with my dad. It was "special" for me to be with him. All of the kids felt the same. He treated us all the same, loving us with a dad's love that could not or cannot ever be denied. We kids knew that Mom took first place; we were a close 2nd. He would have died for us and we knew we had someone that would protect us from the onslaught of any enemy force. Dad weighed 160 lbs. soaking wet....but could take on King Kong and win with one blow (at least we kids thought so). He was truly and sincerely loved by his family.

As much as his family and friends loved my dad, I have to ask the question, "Did EVERYBODY love or even like my dad?" No, I can say with assurance that "Not everyone liked my father." He was a man that could not hold his....tongue when he thought something was wrong or someone was not being truthful and/or respectful. He was one man that was a "man's man." He was one man that was his "woman's man" (my mama's man).

The worst four-letter word that I ever remember dad saying or I might want to remember, is "**hoss**." Yes, "**hoss**" was a word I knew from the very start of listening to my father deal with a liar, a slacker, or someone that wanted to take advantage of a less fortunate one. When Dad would respond to a prideful or ungodly person who tried to put one over on dad, one of his family members, or his co-workers, his first word out of his mouth would be, "Hey, **hoss**, listen to me real clearly; I am going to say this one time……." I hope you get the idea. "Hoss" was a term my dad used to express his feelings for some low-class, conniving hypocrite, or someone that he felt was doing something wrong to his family and/or friends. I didn't hear the term many times, but I do know, when it would be used, he meant business.

Needless to say, however, Dad was held in high esteem with those that believed in God, country and family. However, when a man or woman would tread on the values that those three entities stood for as to his way of thinking, they would get a piece of his mind both in word and, sometime, in deed. Let me explain what this means and explain why Dad might have had a few enemies in his short life on planet earth.

First of all, let me reiterate again and tell you that Dad would lay down his life for his family and his country. He was a mild-mannered man most of the time. However, when someone crossed the line in putting down God, America, his friends, or his family, he could change from a mild-mannered man to a wild-mannered man. Yes…I know that we should not lose our temper or let our emotions get the best of us, but there are such things in life that call for a spiritual response that might be called "righteous anger."

I realize that God is and will be the judge of our attitudes in life. He will make the final decision as to whether we handled the aggravations and provocations appropriately as we deal with situations that confront us. You will see several times in this writing as to how Dad handled "questionable" situations.

In fact, you can be the judge as to how you feel Dad handled these confrontational situations. As you judge him, however, remember that you are not the final judge. In fact, how you feel about it, you will not be judging my dad, but yourself. Dad is with the Father and has already crossed the finish line. You haven't.... but one of these days you most certainly will. Are you ready to make your final appearance before the Judge of all judges? Personally, I will let the blood of Jesus cover me and be my advocate before "the Honorable Judge of the Supreme Court."

My dad worked for every dime he ever placed in his pocket. That sounds far-fetched in that all of us are or were completely dependent when we were very young, incapacitated, and possibly....as we have reached that time in our lives that we would be considered "too old to work for wages." However, Dad made up for all the times his parents had to foot the bill while he was a child. He worked hard as a young boy taking care of the farm picking cotton and cutting wood for the old stove that cooked the meals and warmed the house during the winter months. He fed the hogs, the chickens, and other livestock on the family farm. Going to school was not something to dread;

it was a period of time when he could rest and enjoy learning as well as appreciating the communication with others his age. He did everything he could to help his family meet the tough times in the early 1900s.

Doyle, the younger of two older brothers, had an accident in the old 1941 Plymouth that we had when I was a youngster. I was a passenger in the vehicle and remember the accident because the damage to our vehicle was on the passenger side and I was the one that was injured; not serious enough to go to the hospital, but enough that we had to have the family doctor place some serious bandages on some wounds to my right side.

As with any major fix-up on a house or vehicle, you had to repair it yourself or have someone else to do it that knew more than you did. Working 55 to 70 hours per week on his job, Dad certainly could not repair the vehicle, and was not trained enough to handle a major automobile collision repair. Therefore, dad left our automobile with a local automotive paint and body shop in Abilene, Texas. Prior to leaving the vehicle, he received a formal bid as to the total repair bill on our only personal vehicle we had. The bid included a roll-out price and stated the amount of time it would take to repair the vehicle (one week). Dad had made a substantial down payment before leaving the vehicle with the paint and body shop.

When Dad went back to the shop to pick up the vehicle, he was told that it was not ready and that it would take an additional week to repair it. After waiting an additional week for the vehicle to be repaired, my dad was told that it would be another week and he was quite upset. The automotive shop dealer assured him he would have it ready by the next Friday night when Dad got off work.

Please understand that our family listened to my dad complain about having to wait for the repairs to be done. As we sat around the dinner table at night, Dad would mumble and grumble about the body shop not getting his vehicle out on time. The only other vehicle the family had for picking up groceries and doing other things that needed to be done for our family was the company vehicle (pickup) that was furnished to Dad for being the Foreman/Superintendent for Bailey Bridge Company.

The repair shop owner met Dad on Friday night at his shop. Wanting to be with my dad, my oldest brother and I went with him in the company truck to pick up the vehicle. Dad told me to stay in the truck with my older brother and wait for him to come back. My brother (old enough to drive) could not stay in the vehicle; the anxiety got the best of him. He was afraid that the repair shop owner was going to tell Dad that he had not completed the repair and he knew Dad would be past the point of being just "upset". We had heard enough of the mumbling at home to know that my dad was "loaded for bear" (as one might say). Of course, if my brother went, I was going to tag along.

As we approached the office we could hear the shop owner tell Dad to get out of his office. He was telling my dad that the repairs were going to be much more than what was originally agreed to and that he was not going to release the vehicle unless my dad paid him another substantial sum of money over what was owed after the initial down payment.

I don't remember how much it was, but $2 would have been too much for Dad. My dad did not see Joe or me standing outside the door of the office. Dad did not say anything at first. He hesitated, looked straight in the owner's eyes and grabbed his shirt and literally picked the man up off the floor and told him to give him the keys to the vehicle....now! The word, "hoss" was not used at this time...but I bet my dad thought about it.

The shop owner pleaded for my dad to not hit him and he gave Dad the keys. Dad said, "No, I want a signed statement that this bill is paid in full because I am leaving the money owed on your desk for what the original contract was for....do you understand?" The owner took about 10 minutes to sign the papers stating what my dad wanted him to say. The owner was shaking so bad, Dad had to help him sign it before the ordeal was over.

Dad and I drove home in the company truck and my big brother drove our repaired and freshly painted car home. Dad did not say anything going home. He wept some...but he did not say one thing. He looked over at me as we were pulling into our driveway and said, "Gerald, my boy, don't ever get as mad as what you saw your dad. It is not good for me...and was not good for you. I handled this wrong. Will you forgive me?"

I said, "Uh,huh...I will, dad, but what did you do wrong?" Dad just mumbled something under his breath....something like, "Forgive me, Lord, forgive me!"

At the age of 70, I know now why he asked me to forgive him. I have been in that situation more than once in my life and the picture comes back vividly in my mind every time I am confronted with such ungodly and low-life people.

One of the wonderful things I remember about my dad is that he was not too big to say "I'm sorry"...and he was not too small to say "don't back down and give in to liars, thieves, or anyone who knows to do right, but doesn't."

"Even a child is known by his actions, by whether his conduct is pure and right. Ears that hear and eyes that see—the Lord has made them both" (Proverbs 20:11-12).

Song to call all men for His work:

"Come and join the reapers; all the Kingdom seekers;
Laying down your life to find it in the end.
Come and share the harvest; help to light the darkness,
For the Lord is calling....faithful men."

Text by Twila Paris.

Chapter 4

Building Principles

Deuteronomy 6:5-7, "Love the Lord your God with all your heart and with all your soul and with all your strength. These commandments that I give you today are to be upon your hearts. Impress them on your children. Talk about them when you sit at home and when you walk along the road, when you lie down and when you get up."

The goodness and faithfulness of the Lord is evident. However, the evidence of His care, concerns, and love must not be just read and stored in our hearts; it must be active and alive as part of our being. Our actions truly are more important than mere words.

Dad was a good and honorable man. He spoke often of the importance of putting God first and that what we do, say and even think is known by God. **Here are some important "principles and guidelines for living" that God taught me through my dad:**

1. **Live by the golden rule**...."Love the Lord God with all your soul and might and.....your neighbor as yourself." He lived it. He taught me as I rode with him in the pickup on the weekend to pick up tools, to sharpen saws, to buy clothes for

him and others who might not be able to afford the proper work attire.

I observed my father looking at socks at one of the local general stores (Harry Goltz, Abilene, Texas) and remarking to Mr. Goltz, "If I buy a dozen of these socks, can you give me a much better price?" Dad would use three for himself and pass out the rest of them to the less fortunate workers. Harry Goltz always knew that Dad was getting the socks for others because my dad would buy three or four different sizes at a time. Mr. Goltz was always obliging saying, "Mr. Jay, for you....I will give you a free pair for every two you buy." Respect for my dad was easily recognized. He could be trusted and they knew what Dad said was gospel.

2. **Live by "the Joseph" Principle....**If we are to be a people of principle, let it be a principle of humility, integrity and a will to please the Father.

    "Now Joseph was well-built and handsome, and after a while his master's wife took notice of Joseph and said, 'Come to bed with me!' But he refused. 'With me in charge, 'he told her, 'my master does not concern himself with anything in the house; everything he owns he has entrusted to my care. No one is greater in this house than I am. My master has withheld nothing from me except you, because you are his wife. <u>How then could I do such a wicked thing and sin against God</u>?" (Genesis 39:6b-9).

I have spoken to my brothers, my mother, dad's co-workers, the owner of Bailey Bridge Company, and countless others that were close to my dad. All of them have quickly reported that my daddy never cheated on my mother. Dad was a "man's man" and spoke with great authority (humble, but with strong influence). Was there ever an opportunity for Dad to fall, to look for new pleasures while he was away from his family? No doubt he was presented with temptation, as was Joseph. But my dad would not yield because he did not want to disappoint those who trusted him....nor be found guilty in God's eyes when he stood before Him on judgment day. My dad respected God, family, his country, and life. I praise God that I can take this trait, this unwavering character attribute, and this inherited influence with me to my grave. Along with my dad.....I am determined that I will not be found guilty of trespassing against my neighbor's wife or daughter nor anyone else that God has not ordained as my partner in life.

3. **Learn the "Giving Living" Principle....** Winston Churchill said, "You make a living by getting, but you make a life by giving." What a fascinating precept and truth from a man that had carried a large portion of the world on his shoulders during World War II. He had seen the two major wars take its toll on his family, his country, and the world.

During the beginning of Hitler's march to take the world over one country at a time and, for this unworthy and evil cause, was making a major offensive toward taking over all of Europe and Great Britain, Winston

Churchill became prime minister of Great Britain. Churchill wrote at a later date: "I felt as if I were walking with destiny, and that all my past life had been but a preparation for this hour and for this trial." He made the statement that he "had nothing to offer Great Britain but blood, toil, tears, and sweat." And, the months that followed brought just that…a full measure of blood, toil, sweat and, for sure, many tears. The famous speech made on June 4, 1940, Churchill stated, "We shall not fail. We shall go on to the end…we shall fight in the seas and oceans…we shall fight on the beaches, we shall fight on the landing-grounds, we shall fight in the fields and in the streets, we shall fight in the hills, <u>we shall never surrender</u>…."

Churchill's unwavering call for a "fight to the finish" was echoed around the world and Churchill meant what he said. He turned up everywhere during the height of battle. He defied air-raid alarms and went into the streets as the bombs fell in his beloved country. He visited victims of the air raids and everywhere he went he held up two fingers in a "V for victory" salute. To the people of all the Allied nations, this simple gesture became an inspiring symbol of faith in eventual victory. Hitler was defeated and a new era began for the good of the world.

With such a great hero and military champion in office, who would have ever thought that the citizens of the country he loved so much would not appreciate his leadership? Shortly after Germany surrendered to the Allied Forces, Churchill and his party (Conservative) was defeated by the Labour Party who ran on the promise for sweeping socialistic reforms which appealed to the voters. Memories of the war and the near devastation of Great Britain and the Allied world by the enemy were short-lived. The voters wanted things for themselves in lieu of preparing for tomorrow's enemies that were lurking and waiting in the dark for Great Britain to become weak militarily.

As it was then in Great Britain, so it is now in America. The enemies, the radical Muslim, the terrorist are waiting for a weak military force by America and they will try, as they have in the past, to put this great country to its knees. So far, the enemies' tactics have worked and their plan to take over the world, including the United States, has become a possibility. Nowhere have we seen a call for a strengthening of our military and equipment....and only seeing a "what is in it for me" attitude exhibited and heard in the news media. "Bailouts and Hand-outs" are becoming a trend throughout American culture (politically and personally). For many Americans, the idea that there are some bad and evil-minded people that wish for our blood is not relevant, justified, nor possible in today's society. They have a "get it now" philosophy, in lieu of a "giving attitude" to meet the needs of others before self. Only God can cause attitudes to change. Only God can intervene and cause hearts to turn toward Him and His ways. Our God is a radical God. He demands and commands that we are to "present ourselves living sacrifices that are holy and acceptable before Him."

Dad was my Winston Churchill, my hero, my champion that would place his life on the line for his family, his God, and his friends. He depicted the Churchill character of "speaking softly and swinging a big stick." He never yelled at us; he never "spanked" us with an intent to destroy our confidence in him. He never disciplined for no reason. He was fair, honest, and reliable in completing the chores and responsibilities in which he knew to do and what he said he would do (whether to buy us candy and soda pop for our chores, or strongly discipline for our failing to do what we were supposed to do…or doing what we were not to do). We, my brothers and sister, respected him for his consistency and his unyielding charter of making our lives count for our sake as well as others.

Hymn to Search the Soul:

"Search me, O God, and know my heart today; Try me,
O Savior, know my thoughts, I pray.
See if there be some wicked way in me; Cleanse me from
every sin and set me free.
I praise Thee, Lord, for cleansing me from sin; Fulfill
Thy Word and make me pure within.
Fill me with fire where once I burned with shame; Grant
my desire to magnify Thy name.
O Holy Ghost, revival comes from Thee; Send a revival,
start the work in me.
Thy Word declares Thou wilt supply our need; For bless-
ings now, O Lord, I humbly plead."

Text by J. Edwin Orr; based on Psalm 139:23.

＊＊

Chapter 5

Building Memories

"Whoever loves discipline loves knowledge, but he who hates correction is stupid" (Proverbs 12:1).

Dad had his days of ups and downs; but most of the time the downs involved others. His time of depression and being down did not ever center in on himself. His love for family, friends and co-workers overshadowed any disagreements, any discouragement, or any tragedies in his life. His concern for what was going on in the lives of others sometimes overwhelmed any troubles or disheartening moments that were going on in the immediate "Jay Cumby" family. A quote from an old gentleman that I was listening to several years ago was, "Worry is like a rocking chair….It will give you something to do, but it won't get you any where!" Really, this is true…but the fact is, the best of us worry at some time or another. As a Christian, I want to say that "I don't worry, I just have major concerns." Who is kidding whom? We can paint a rosy picture all around "worry"….but, in the end, worry is still in the picture.

Dad always was the one that took the lead in making sure that his workers were properly rewarded for their skills and hard work. Please understand, Dad would not have a man on the payroll that was a "slacker" (lazy), a thief, a poor father or husband, or one who did not take care of his bills if he was capable. Dad did not have any problem "reprimanding and strongly encouraging" an employee when his work was not up-to-par or an employee who failed to take care of his family. My dad seemed to have the drive of an Army Sergeant and the sting of a Military General. He did not tolerate poor workmanship or laziness. Therefore, those workers that worked "with" him knew the rules and policies of Bailey Bridge Company and tried to follow those rules as much as possible. Many of the workers had worked "with" Dad for as many years as he had been a Bridge Foreman (Superintendent). They knew that Dad was a man that required a lot….but gave a lot in return.

I heard the stories about my dad from the workers and their wives. What these stories told….was that my dad was an honest, hard-working, and compassionate man that would give the shirt off his back (literally) to make sure that his fellow workers and their families had their basic needs met. Some of the stories will be told in this writing. However, most of the stories that will be told are ones that I know are true with no exaggeration….for most of these stories are experiences with my dad that I observed, heard, and witnessed…from close range.

With Dad being the superintendent of Bailey Bridge Company, he would move to the nearest town where his company won the bid for the bridges and road construction for the county or state. Sometimes we moved with him if the project was going to be for

4 months or more. From the 1st grade until the 8th, I attended 9 different schools. From Stephenville, Texas to Channing, Texas to Childress, Texas with our main base being Abilene, Texas, we would move with Dad because we wanted to be near him. However, many times we would not move from our rented home in Abilene and we would only see my dad on the weekends. Mother waited patiently for her man to come home….and we were excited to know that it was Friday because my daddy would be home late that night until late Sunday night.

If it were too far for Dad to make it home in 3 to 5 hours on Friday, then we would move with him. We would live in a rented house as near to Dad's work as possible. Usually the rented homes were small and inconvenient. However, they were always clean and had a fresh smell; Mom would make sure of that.

It was normal for Dad to have at least 4-6 workers coming home with him when he worked too far from home base. Of course, their families were as excited to see them as we were our precious dad. These workers were the bridge construction crew that moved around with my dad. However, Dad would always hire some men from the area where the bridges and construction projects were being built.

Every chapter must come to an end. As long as a chapter covers an important point in which our goal or objective is met, then it is relevant. I think you will see how relevant the above chapters are as you read, hear and see (picture in your mind) the story of "the bridge builder." For at the age of 13,...on April 22, 1955, my world, as I knew it then, was turned upside down.

In the first chapter, I spoke of six words that my sister-in-law, Joe's wife, communicated to me that fateful day at the track meet. **Those six words she said to me that rocked my boat, shattered my dreams at the time, and broke my young spirit, were,** ***"Gerald, your dad was killed today!"***

Shocked and stunned, I wilted in my coach's arms. For my security blanket, my hero, my faithful "knight in shining armor".......my precious dad was killed when he accidentally fell from a bridge he was building...and my world of peace and joy came crashing down.

Hymn from the Author of Peace:

"When peace like a river attendeth my way,
When sorrows like sea billows roll,
Whatever my lot, Thou hast taught me to say,
'It is well, it is well with my soul.'

Though Satan should buffet, tho' trials should come,
Let this blest assurance control,
That Christ has regarded my helpless estate,
And hath shed His own blood for my soul.

My sin—O, the bliss of his glorious thought,
My sin—not in part but the whole,
Is nailed to the cross and I bear it no more,
Praise the Lord, Praise the Lord, O my soul!

And, Lord, haste the day when the faith shall be sight,
The clouds be rolled back as a scroll,
The trump shall resound and the Lord shall descend,
'Even so'—it is well with my soul.
It is well...with my soul...
It is well, it is well with my soul."

Text by Haratio G. Spafford.

Chapter 6

Building Bridges For
A Journey Home

"If a man dies, will he live again? All the days of my hard service I will wait for my renewal to come. You will call and I will answer you; you will long for the creature your hands have made. Surely then will you count my steps but not keep track of my sin. My offenses will be sealed up in a bag; you will cover over my sin" (Job 14:14-17).

"Blessed are they whose transgressions are forgiven, whose sins are covered. Blessed is the man whose sin the Lord will never count against him" (Romans 4:7-8).

It is hard to imagine what runs through the mind of a 13 year old when he has been told that his hero has been killed. I don't imagine it, I know. It is one of the most dreadful feelings and the worst nightmare in which you realize is not something that will be gone when you wake up in the morning. I had been hurt before with disappointments and discouraging losses, but never like this.

I am a 70 year old that has gone through about every traumatic situation one might imagine. I have been through my sister's tragic loss of her only son (she backed over him when he was only 18 months old). My sister died of cancer at the age of 62. My nephew (Leahman Ray) was like a son to my future wife (Sherry) and I. However, when the news was explained to me about my dad, I was placed in a holding pattern. I was having a bad dream; I would wake up soon; my mom would come and tell me it wasn't true; and, my dad would awaken me and take me in his arms and say, "Don't you know, son, I will never leave you!"

After being told of the accident and my dad's death, I was placed in a vehicle and driven straight home. With many of my family members and neighbors in the front yard and porch, I could not talk through my panic and tears. I walked through the crowd of deeply saddened and weeping family members and tried to find my mom. I could hear her from the front room as she was crying out to the God she knew but didn't understand. She was crying out for her family to tell her it was not so. I made my way into the room and bed where my mom was in a traumatic state; pain beyond what one could imagine. Her glance toward me was one that I had never seen before from her. It was like, "My son...my boy...I don't understand...It's not real... it's not fair!" She opened her arms up to me and we cried together for at least 20 minutes. My little brothers, Randy, 9 years old, and Tony, 5, were crying because we were crying. Like any little fellows that were witnessing all the sadness in the home that evening, they could not help but cling to Mom and cry out....as their little world had been shattered, also. They knew that if Mom was sad and crying it can't be good.

I have had some conversations with Randy and Tony over the last few years and they tell me that they hardly remember their daddy or any of his particular traits because they were so young when the tragedy happened. However, because my brothers (all of them) have traits like my mom and dad (love of God, family, and country), they had to pick up much of the good and wholesome truths exhibited by their parents. In other words, they might not remember Dad, but their sub-conscious minds picked up the love and solid foundational truths my dad left with all of us. Today, my brothers....Doyle, Randy, and Tony love the Lord with all their heart. No doubt, their dad and mom would be proud of their status in life; especially their strong leadership abilities and their deep commitment to family, friends, God, and country.

When my older brothers and sister (all married) came over to peel me out of my mother's arms that tragic evening, I ran through the house and out the front door toward a field just west of our home. As I was running, I was stumbling over the plowed rows of dirt that made up about a 50-acre farm area. There were no fences and I made it to the middle of the field and fell to my knees due to exhaustion and panic, held my fist up to a God that I really did not personally know, and cried, "I hate you...I hate you. What have you done to my mom? What have you done to my daddy? I hate you...I hate you!"

I really don't remember who found me in the field, but I just remember waking up in my bed in the middle of the night and hearing my mother and family weeping. I again cried myself to sleep.

The next two days were gripping, and memorable; memorable because the memory of my dad in the casket has played over and over in my mind over the years. The funeral, the images, the songs, the preacher's message was like a recording that was part of me as I waded through the next few weeks. Mom cried a lot, but she was strong, too. I don't know whether it was for me or all of her children, but she kept saying, "I don't understand it, but we will make it."

And she, throughout the rest of her life, lived up to her statement. This God-fearing, lovely, precious, hard-working mother of three children at home provided the strength and courage that can only be understood when you see the picture of our family at a later date. She was more than a "Bridge Builder"; she was a "World Changer." In my mind and in my judgment, nobody has changed the world in which she lived and breathed..more than my mom. She changed it because she "held on" and "held fast" to God's unchanging principles; that of living the godly life and not just talking about it. She "walked the walk"... not just "talked the talk."

In my mom's kitchen, there was a picture that said a lot without saying anything. The picture was of an elderly gray-headed woman with wrinkles, sitting at a small kitchen table, with head bowed. In front of her was a bowl of soup. To anyone looking at the picture they knew that this woman gave thanks for the provisions given to her by a God that loved her much. With no one else around, just she and God, she was willing to give praise to the One who cared for her. I think of that picture quite often. I see in the picture, of course, my mom. She did not need an audience to give praise to the Creator of life and the one that "holds tomorrow." Was she a "bridge builder?" Indeed and in deeds she was.

Any one that knew my mom certainly knew that she was a "silent partner" with God. She was sincere in her love for her God, her Savior, her family, and her country. I really think she had her priorities in line with what God had in mind when he said, "Love the Lord thy God, with all your heart, with all your soul, and with all your might (strength)."

Mom was more than a mother, sister, or a loving neighbor. She was a friend to her children and to her neighbors. She was one that kids knew that they were loved when they were held. She was one that God knew that He was loved when she bowed her head and gave thanks.

She was building bridges until her dying breath...in which she crossed over that threshold into God's Kingdom. She taught others how to die. With dignity she lived and with dignity she died. I watched her breathe her last. I saw her reach for eternity in her last hour. It was like she was saying, "It is finished." Her life was over, but her bridge building was not.

I still cross treacherous waters, deep ravines, and bottomless pits with Mom on my mind. How would she handle the situation? How would she react to such a discouraging word from the doctor? How would she take on Goliath with a slingshot as bad news came into our lives? I can see now, bridge building doesn't stop when life is over. Bridge building is not just what we touch and feel; it is what we use in times of storms and torrential rains on the day of the parade.

Hymn of Peace and Commitment:

"Far away in the depths of my spirit tonight rolls a
melody sweeter than psalm;
In celestial like strains in unceasingly falls o'er my soul
like an infinite calm.

What a treasure I have in this wonderful peace, buried
deep in the heart of my soul;
So secure that no power can mine it away, while the
years of eternity roll.

I am resting tonight in this wonderful peace, resting
sweetly in Jesus' control;
For I'm kept from all danger by night and by day, and
His glory is flooding my soul.

And I think when I rise to that city of peace, where the
Author of peace I shall see,
That one strain of the song which the ransomed will
sing, in that heavenly kingdom shall be:

O my soul, are you here without comfort or rest,
marching down the rough pathway of time? Make
the Savior your friend before the shadows grow dark;
Oh, accept this sweet peace so sublime.

Peace! Peace! Wonderful peace, coming down from the
Father above;
Sweep over my spirit forever, I pray, In fathomless billows of love."

Text by W.D. Cornell.

Chapter 7

Building On The Rock

"One man gives freely, yet gains even more; another withholds unduly, but come to poverty" (Proverbs 11:24).

My dad and mom were givers. They gave when giving wasn't popular. They gave not to be seen or heard, but because of the need. Not because of the need that was evident by those that received their gift, but because of the need placed in their heart to be a blessing.

There are some in life that struggle with the idea of giving more than they are getting. There are some that have a hard time with the giving principle because they can't see past their own need. They can't see the truth in the Scripture as to the fact that generous men will prosper while greedy men will lose what is gained.

My dad and mom lived the giving principle. They gave if it meant going into debt. They gave if it meant that they had to struggle to make ends meet. They gave because their heart was touched by the greatest Giver of all times…a loving and faithful God. I have seen dad give his last pair of socks that did not have a hole in them. I have seen mom give a gift at Christmas time to children, neighbors, and relatives when she did not have money to pay for a cab to go to the grocery store.

This is not an exaggeration, it is a fact that I experienced for myself.

Why did they do it? I have asked that on many occasions. Why suffer when it is not practical? Why do things for others when the "others" were much better off than yourself? The answer is found in the Scripture, "The desire of the righteous ends only in good, but the hope of the wicked only in wrath" (Proverbs 11:23). Dad and Mom's desire was to "be good and do good." Their heart had been tenderized by the Giver of Life. Their desire for treasures here on earth was stifled when Jesus came in and made priorities properly aligned as to what is important and what is "trivial".

One Christmas, I was wishing for (wanting) a bicycle more than anything else in all the world (my thoughts). All the young boys in the 3rd grade had new bicycles. I had been given hand-me-down tricycles and bicycles from the time I was old enough to say "Udn, udn" (the sound that a vehicle makes) until then…about two months before Christmas (1950). The temptation of a new bike was more than my mind could comprehend. I daydreamed about a new bike and at night I laid awake just thinking about this new bicycle that I saw in the Sears Roebuck catalog. The bike had a light on the front and special handlebars that was the talk of the boys at school. The bike that I had been riding for the last two years was about a 10 year old 24" reconditioned "Hawthorne", without fenders. The wheels were a little warped and a few spokes were missing, but it was my treasure…until I saw the one in the catalog.

I really did not make Dad and Mom aware of my desire to have this new bike. However, I had removed the page in the catalog that had the special deal on this "special bike" and placed it on my chest of drawers where my little brother and I slept. Every morning and every evening I would read about this bicycle and looked at the distinct description and picture of the bike until I imagined myself riding to school on the new wheels "Santa" had brought me...for being good (I was now old enough and mature enough to know where the real "Santa things" came from and how they arrived at our home).

One afternoon about 3 weeks before Christmas I happened to notice that the door of the detached garage in the back of our home was locked. It never had a lock on it before and, since I had played in the old garage when it was raining, I knew that there was a reason Dad had placed a chain and lock on the door. My thoughts were, "What was in the garage that my dad did not want me to see and why now?" I asked my dad why the lock was on the door and he responded with a very adamant reply... "Son, just stay away from the garage." Of course, my curiosity got me....I had to try and get into the garage. I waited until my parents went to the grocery store and I took a piece of lumber and pried open the door enough that I could see what I never intended to see. I saw the bike of my dreams, put together with fancy handle bar grips and all, right there in the garage. The real bike from the Sears Roebuck catalog was more than a dream...it was going to become a reality. I wanted to scream "Yes"; but my anxiety and joy quickly turned to something that I never thought would happen. Now, how would I ever keep "the secret" a secret? How would I hold my expression of jubilant elation down until Christmas morning when the bike would be parked under the Christmas tree waiting for my visual "surprised and jubilant" response in front of the family?

Several times in those 3 weeks Mom would ask me what was wrong and why the gloom and doom look on my face. It was the longest 3 weeks of my life and they weren't pleasant ones either. I worried about disappointing my dad and mom if they knew that I knew what they had in store for me at Christmas time. I worried about my betrayal of trust by disobeying my dad's command to "stay away from the garage."

For an obvious reason I was not a happy camper after my discovery. The bike was not the issue; my spirit was the issue. My excitement turned to despair and my countenance and child-like spirit became a spirit of disappointment and discontent. What I was going to get for Christmas was not because I was "good" any longer. I was the "bad" boy that had disobeyed his father. My eyes were open to what was "good and evil." Does this sound like a familiar story?

I was a miserable wreck for those 3 weeks….and beyond. I had a hard time in those few weeks in school before Christmas. One side of me was saying, "But the bike….remember the bike." The other side of me was saying, "You ate the apple and disobeyed your father."

Well, I wasn't kicked out of the Garden of Eden… nor my home. However, I did come to the realization that disobedience has its consequences. I received my new bike on Christmas morning and I acted like I was surprised and happy....but deep down I was a wretched wreck.

I never did tell Dad about my act of disobedience. I did tell my mom later that next year. She put her arm around me and said, "Well, Gerald, did you learn anything from this?.....and, by the way, I think your dad knew that you knew what was in the garage. I will let you be the one to tell him."

I never told my dad what I did. I mean....I never confessed my sin to him. He died less than 5 years later and I still had not confessed up to my wretched act. I had failed my earthly father....and I had failed my heavenly Father. Now you know why I was so angry with God the day my dad died. I had my sin ever present before me...and now I had no time to ask my father to forgive me for disobeying him.

Hymn of Freedom and Purpose:

"Years I spent in vanity and pride, caring not my Lord
     was crucified,
Knowing not it was for me He died on Calvary.
Mercy there was great and grace was free, pardon there
     was multiplied to me,
There my burdened soul found liberty—at Calvary.

By God's Word at last my sin I learned—Then I trem-
     bled at the law I'd spurned,
Till my guilty soul imploring turned to Calvary.

Now I've given to Jesus every thing, now I gladly own
     Him as my King,
Now my raptured soul can only sing of Calvary.

O the love that drew salvation's plan! O the grace that
     brought it down to man!
O the mighty gulf that God did span….at Calvary.
Mercy there was great and grace was free, pardon there
     was multiplied to me,
There my burdened soul found liberty—at Calvary."

Text by William R. Newell.

Chapter 8

Building For Heavenly Treasures

"Oh wretched man that I am, who shall deliver me from the body of this death? I thank God through Jesus Christ our Lord. So then with the mind I myself serve the law of God; but with the flesh the law of sin" (Romans 7:24-25a), NKJ.

The freedom from the burden of guilt that I carried for being a "disobedient and deceiving" son was given to me when I accepted the fact that I could be forgiven by my heavenly Father through Jesus Christ...who gave His life for me and became a sin offering for my awful transgression. I needed a daddy to hold me and say, "I love you and forgive you" as a 9 year old kid. I needed a daddy as a 13 year old to tell me that I am forgiven for my transgressions. Dad was gone. Dad was no longer available for me to tell of my transgressions...and I was more than miserable; I was on the verge of a total breakdown due to my failure to ask for forgiveness.

The cliché, "confession is good for the soul" is a truth, not just a trite phrase. However, it is only a "half-truth." It is not just good for the soul, but body, mind and spirit (the whole person). I needed to be released from a prison that I had placed myself in. All I had to do was tell my dad and there is no doubt that I would have been forgiven. My procrastination and my delay in "coming clean" with my deception with my dad caused me to blame myself for my dad's death. I thought that God had caused his death to get back at me for my willful disobedience and my willful failure to confess my sin of disobedience and deception to my father.

Little did I know at the time of my dad's death was the time that the Holy Spirit started working gently and tenderly with me. I can't tell you how hard I fought against the Holy Spirit's convicting power. I fought Him "tooth and toe-nail" (literally). My teeth ached and my fingernails were chewed to the quick. I was a teen-age mess going down for the count.

I knew that my dad was in heaven and I knew that I needed to still talk to him. I did not know how and I did not understand that there was a great gulf fixed between my world and God's Kingdom. My sister and brother-in-law must have seen my plight. They picked me up at my home and took me Sunday after Sunday to a church where I heard the Word of God preached....vigorously. Invitations to accept God's forgiveness through His Son were shunned by a calloused heart; not hardened, but calloused and crusty. Thank God that His Spirit and Love did not let up on me. In August of the same year that my dad died (1955), I humbled myself and confessed my transgressions before Him. I wept and cried out to the God who created me....and He released me of the guilt that was trampling my body, soul, and spirit. For some reason that I did not understand then and my finite mind of today still does not understand, I was free of the guilt that had plagued me concerning the disobedient experience with my earthly father in which I never had confessed.

The fact that my sins have been forgiven and forgotten by my heavenly father gave me a "freedom" I will never be able to explain with words. Human intellect cannot express what is heavenly wisdom. A spiritual experience cannot be understood by someone that is trying to understand it with only human intellect...no matter how "smart" he or she is. That is why a person that tries to calculate all the facts of life and come to a conclusion as to what is real and what is not cannot get an answer that he or she understands. Without the personal experience with the Savior, one cannot figure out the importance of grace and faith in the salvation that is offered to everyone who desires to believe. The unbeliever's concept as to what Jesus has done for mankind does not calculate. It is beyond what the human mind can contemplate. Only if we come as little children with an uninhibited act of humility can we see why Jesus did what He did. He came down from His father's house (heaven) and made a way "once and for all" for those who choose to follow His way of "faith" without seeing with human eyes. Jesus himself said to Thomas, "Thomas, you believe because you have seen. Blessed are those who have not seen yet believe" (John 20:29), NKJ paraphrased.

With this in mind, I must ask this at this time. Have you, the reader, humbled yourself before the One who created you and asked for forgiveness of your sin? The Bible clearly states, "All have sinned and come short of the glory of God." It is a fact that "the payment for sin is death." However, "the gift God offers is eternal life.....

through Jesus Christ, our Lord." There is no other way. There is no "tolerant or cultural issue" here. It is "the Way, the Truth, and the Life."

In the movie *Forest Gump,* Forest made a simple statement in his slow and pronounced Southern drawl, "I may not be very smart, but I know when it's raining." With that in mind, Gerald Cumby may not be really, really intelligent, but I know where I am going after I complete this life on earth. I am a man that knows that I consciously have made mistakes in my life. Some of those mistakes were simply "dumb" mistakes. Some were quite "foolish and immature" while some were down-right (I hate to say it) stupid. Stupid, in my book, is worse than dumb…because it carries the connotation that one knows better, but keeps doing the same mistake over and over again ("Stupid is as stupid does").

It is evident that the man that looks at himself in the mirror and thinks he has all the answers to the problems of life…is a man that is not facing reality. He knows better than to shake his fist at the God of the Universe who has made it possible for a positive afterlife experience, but over and over again, he rejects the Maker of life….the One that has made heaven possible through His Son's death on the cross.

Life is short and death will come to all. We must choose to believe that there is an afterlife or there is not. It is a personal choice. I choose to believe that there is more to this life than a few years of living. There is a God who made it all and has a place for us if we choose to "confess with our mouth the Lord Jesus and believe in our heart that God raised Him from the dead, we will be saved." I urge the reader to accept God's Word as fact. The first step is to either "have it your way" or "have it God's way." I have every reason to believe that God's way is the only way since it ends in a positive light. A "this life and this life only" concept....has a path that leads to nowhere...ending in the bottomless pit.

"Choose you this day whom you will serve. As for me and my house, we will serve the Lord" (Joshua 24:15).

Hymn of Redemption:

"I have a song I love to sing, since I have been redeemed,
Of my Redeemer, Savior, King, since I have been
redeemed.

I have a Christ who satisfies, since I have been redeemed,
To do His will my highest prize, since I have been
redeemed.

I have a witness bright and clear, since I have been
redeemed,
Dispelling every doubt and fear, since I have been
redeemed.

I have a home prepared for me, since I have been
redeemed,
Where I shall dwell eternally, since I have been
redeemed.
Since I have been redeemed, I will glory in His name….
Since I have been redeemed, I will glory in my Savior's
name.

Text by Edwin O. Excell

Chapter 9

Building Faith

"His (David's) servants asked him, 'Why are you acting this way? While the child was alive, you fasted and wept, but now that the child is dead, you get up and eat!' He answered, 'While the child was still alive, I fasted and wept. I thought, 'who knows? The Lord may be gracious to me and let the child live.' But now that he is dead, why should I fast? Can I bring him back again? I will go to him, but he will not return to me" (2 Samuel 12:21-23).

I have thought about Dad quite often throughout my life. I do not dwell on any negative thing that I or someone else might reflect about him. I choose to "center in on" only those experiences with Dad that were positive and uplifting. One might think that if I remember and write about the pain of my Dad's death and the experiences that immediately followed this tragedy, I cannot be dwelling on "just the positive." I beg to differ with you if you feel that way. I look back on Dad's death, Mom's plight of having to be a dad and mom to "us boys" after losing Dad, the crying and the depth of grief we went through for months at a time, and I see it as a "valley of death" that we had to go through to get to the top of the mountain on the other side. I see that the

Word of God is so challenging, so convicting, so penetrating....and yet so right (absolute truth) that I can't help but believe and trust that "all things work together for good to them that love God and are called according to His purpose."

Dad's death was not "good" when one looks at it from the human standpoint. However, let me tell you that neither the final second of life, nor the final lap of reflection before death will measure our depth of love for life, our family, or our God; nor will only the good things that happen to us throughout our life prepare us for our journey home. Preparation for the journey home has to be made with some regret or reflective moments of sad occurrences in life. I know that Dad and Mom made preparation for their journey home and did it with a lot of sad experiences as they walked through the valley. But remember, it is a walk that we go <u>through</u> as we walk through the valley of life. We don't stay in the valley. We go through it even if the walk causes us to get some deep wounds that will affect us every day of our life.

As mentioned previously, Mom was a shining example of how we are to live our lives. She lived a long and highly effective life in which her children and grandchildren can be very proud. She was strong in her faith and her desire to leave a legacy of stability as to maintaining godly values. One might say, however, that my dad, on the other hand, did not get a fair share of living since he had to leave so much on the table when he was called home.

It has been stated by one person without godly wisdom, "Your dad was the best man I have ever known…...and I don't understand a God that would not let this man live a much longer life where he could be a great servant to God and his fellow man." I don't have a definitive answer for this person without sounding like I am irrational and impractical. All I know is that when I get to meet my father again in a heaven that is absolutely more than I can ever imagine, I will not be disappointed in my life, my dad's legacy, nor God's method or plan to accomplish His goals and objectives for His creation. I just know that God is omnipotent, omniscient, and can do anything He wants to in order to gather the Bride of Christ to an eternal home. Anytime a tragedy happens to one of God's children, I know that my Lord God has a means of attack to make sure that His original plan to redeem mankind stays on track. His Word is always faithful and true.

The final impact on others as to how Dad lived and died will not be felt by what we see and feel as we head home on our last lap. I just know that many lives were touched by his compassion and his willingness to put others' needs ahead of his own. His love for life, his friends, his co-workers, his family, and his God and Savior will be a trademark that will be carried from one generation to another. This will be communicated from one father in the Cumby family to another little one, and that little one to his offspring some years later. Keeping track of time is not as important as keeping track of loyal and dedicated members of a family that know what it means to live life to the fullest....but doing it without sacrificing moral and godly principles.

I can say this without hesitation or doubt, "Every one of my siblings (four brothers and one sister) gave or have given their lives to Jesus." They each had their problems and, like any other person, dealt with various sins in their life. They, however, kept the faith in knowing where they were and are going after this life is over. I am proud to say that I will be able to see my family in heaven and all will be well as we fellowship with one another while gathering around the throne room worshipping the King of Kings and Lord of Lords.

Hymn of Faith and Patience:

I will meet you in the morning, just inside the Eastern
    Gate;
Then be ready, faithful pilgrim, lest with you it be too
    late.

I will meet you in the morning, just inside the Eastern
    Gate over there;

If you hasten off to glory, linger near the Eastern Gate,
For I'm coming in the morning, so you'll not have
    long to wait.

Keep your lamps all trimmed and burning, for the
    Bridegroom watch and wait;
He'll be with us at the meeting, just inside the
    Eastern Gate.

O, the joy of that glad meeting, with the saints who for
    us wait!
What a blessed, happy meeting, just inside the Eastern
    Gate.

Chorus: I will meet you in the morning
I will meet you in the morning

Just inside the Eastern Gate over there;
I will meet you in the morning
I will meet you in the morning
I will meet you in the morning over there.

Text written by Isaiah G. Martin

Chapter 10

Building Truth And Trust

"For the Lord gives wisdom, and from his mouth come knowledge and understanding. He holds victory in store for the upright, he is a shield to those whose walk is blameless, for he guards the course of the just and protects the way of his faithful ones. Then you will understand what is right and just and fair—every good path. For wisdom will enter your heart, and knowledge will be pleasant to your soul. Discretion will protect you, and understanding will guard you" (Proverbs 2:6-11).

Dad was quite a man. He was one of those men that would come from a funeral and show sincere tears and react with genuine compassion when families were in grief. He would hear a story about a family losing a spouse or child to a murderous low-life...and be weeping and angry at the same time. Yet, when someone crossed the line with him as to trying to hurt his family or take advantage of them in any way, he was a giant of a man in a 160-pound "earth suit."

My sister, Pat (the only girl of the six siblings), was her daddy's girl. He protected that girl with his heart, soul, and body. To hear Pat speak of Dad, you would not have to hear what she was saying; for her eyes could easily tell the story of how she felt about him. They would brighten up and dance with an array of dazzling colors and stars by just mentioning her "daddy". He was her hero. He was the knight in shining armor when Pat needed attention and a hug to lift her spirits.

Several young men had their eyes on Pat. However, like most short romances, the luster of the new honey of her life quickly diminished with time.

When Pat was probably around 19 and out of high school, there was a young man that started courting her. He was a few years older (probably 24 or 25) and was a handsome "dude." From what I remember, he was quite a gentleman when calling on her. For the sake of incrimination and possibly hurting others, I will call him "Don". Don asked my dad if it was all right to date Pat. He would tell Dad where and what they had planned on doing each time he dated her. After about six months of courtship, the young man asked for Pat's hand in marriage. I remember Dad crying when Pat came in and told him that she really felt that this was the man God intended for her to be with the rest of her life. Dad consented and plans were in the making for a wedding.

In an earlier chapter, I mentioned that Dad would work out of town through the week and come home on the weekends when it was practical and reasonable. Dad left work with two of his men in his company pickup one Friday afternoon. They had finished a major concrete pour of a bridge that they had been working on in West Texas. The trip back to Abilene, our home base, went through Sweetwater, Texas…the home of the young man (Don) who had asked Pat to marry him.

While stopped at a light on Highway 80 in down-town Sweetwater, Dad noticed the soon-to-be son-in-law standing at the corner of the street waiting for the light to change. However, next to his side were a young lady and a 2-3 year old little boy. Dad pulled his pickup over to the curb and walked quite briskly over to Don. Don looked startled when he saw my dad and tried to get the lady and boy to go into a nearby store. Dad confronted Don (knowing that there was something definitely wrong with the scene) and point-blank asked him who the lady and boy were....in the lady's presence. Don, sheepishly and with a blank look, stated that this was his wife. Dad, with a quiver in his lip, quietly asked the lady and son to go into the nearest department store because he had to take care of some business with her husband.

According to the two men that were in the pickup across the street, my dad let the lady and her son disappear into the nearest store and then took Don around the corner where an arm went up against the throat of this deceitful and lying hypocrite. Don, begging for mercy, begged Dad to not cause prob-lems with his wife and son. Dad told him that if he ever (emphasis on ever) saw him within 20 miles of Abilene, Texas, as long as he (my dad) was alive, he (Don) better understand that there would be conse-quences...and those consequences were more than Don needed to think about. He also told him to never contact Pat or my mom again. If he did, he would have the detectives in Abilene all over his case and it would not be pretty.

I think the last statement Dad made to Don was, "Do you understand what I mean....Hoss?"

I remember that Friday night like it was yesterday. I was about 10 years old at the time. Dad came in that evening with tears in his eyes and asked Pat and Mom to come with him to the back bedroom. I could hear Pat and Mom crying. Pat was saying that "It was not true."

However, after she could not cry anymore (4 days later), she came in and hugged Daddy asking if he was going to be all right. According to Mom, Dad had not gone back to work on Monday and Tuesday because he was so upset about it all. I think Pat matured more in those 4 days than she had the previous 19 years. Because of mom's wise counseling and encouragement, she understood her daddy's love and concern for his pride and joy of life.

We never saw Don again. I think he understood the consequences and, if he is still alive today, has probably never stopped in Abilene on his way to points eastward. Dad had that "Hey, hoss, do you understand what I mean" aura about him. Soaking wet, he was a "flyweight" at best. However, he was a heavy weight in our books.... because he meant what he said and he never backed down on principles and the basic character qualities of which God would approve. He was a man in whom a young boy probably would not appreciate such "great love" of a daddy until he was older and placed in similar situations. My dad was not the typical dad; he was quite "unique in his technique" as a parent, as a daddy, and as a husband. Mom was truly the heart of the home and Dad was the one that kept the heart beating.

The question of the day would be, "What is it that places within the heart of a man a desire to protect his family with his life (if necessary) from the onslaught of the enemy?" It is not a gift or a talent God gives to whomever He desires. Although God plays a big part in keeping his creation on track and in line with the principles lined out in His Word, it is not His intention to make or force a person to become what he or she does not desire to be. God has given His Word and His directions, but it is up to man to read the directions and then follow them. Just as a dad tries to put a swing set together that he buys his children for Christmas, he must follow directions as he places every piece delicately in place to complete the product. Without the directions and without the will to follow the directions, that swing set will be a nightmare for him to complete by Christmas morning (believe me, I know this is true from personal experience).

The Word of God is that way. God desires that we keep our lives in line with His Word. However, reading the Word is not enough; we must do the Word and follow His directions if we are to accomplish in our lives what God has desired from us. In fact, His plans are not to "disable" us when we fail him, but to "enable" us to complete our lives here on earth with a will to be complete in Him. It is left up to us to choose His way or the world's way. The world's directions lead us to eternal damnation and God's directions lead us to eternal life. Dad chose to obey God and God chose Dad to be the man (His creation) He intended him to be from the beginning. Dad loved much and Dad gave his all to make sure his family knew exactly that. We understood that he would die protecting and taking care of his family. God was first.....and his family far ahead of what was in 3rd place.

Learning Principles from Chapter 10:

1. **Trust by Testing**— What looks good "close up" might be a monster when observed from a distance. With that in mind, it is imperative that all persons trying to enter your family's or one of your family's world are thoroughly checked out via one-on-one conversations, speaking to friends and family of the new "want-to-be" family friend, getting the person to give you their views on politics...and yes, religious beliefs. One of the most expedient ways to discover the "sincerity" of a person is to have him/her over for dinner and find out if they are open to their views on their religious beliefs and practices. Another thing that any family (dad or mom, brother or sister) needs to do in trying to find out about a person entering their family's world is to remember that, "If you question them....you should be willing and expect to be questioned by those you question." In fact, if they are not willing to find out what is going on in your family, they are not interested in what matters most in a long-term relationship....trust.

2. **FEAR Is Not Always a "Negative" Character Flaw**—Pride can be negative or positive. Pride

can be a selfish and an ungodly trait. Lucifer (Satan) was ejected from heaven due to his pride and thought of being equal to or above God. God is "God Almighty" and He alone is to be praised. Pride, however, in family, country, or in work achievements can be a very positive and commendable feeling and action. FEAR is like pride. Fear of the consequences of one's actions can cause conflict and negative emotions in one's life. When we place fear on others or ourselves by our thoughts and actions, it can be a detriment to future decisions for both others and ourselves. By making decisions that go against the Word of God, by not obeying God's laws and precepts, and by willfully, deceitfully, and selfishly promoting evil ways, one might not fear God...but in reality, really should fear the Almighty, the Judge of All Creation.

On the other hand, "godly fear" can be a commendable trait. Deuteronomy 6:13 states that we should "Fear the Lord your God, serve Him..." and Deuteronomy 31:12 says that we should "...learn to fear the Lord your God." Why should we fear God? Because those who know Jesus Christ as Savior, need to understand God's definition of fearing God. His definition is found in His Word.... "To fear God is to hate evil" (Proverbs 8:13).

If God hates evil, we certainly should hate evil with a passion. Don, the lying, conniving guy, who deceived my sister and my family, thought he had out-witted the Cumby family with his good manners and gentlemanly actions. He did not fear the consequences because he thought he was "too smart" for my dad and my sister. One thing for sure, Don's deceitful confidence quickly turned to fear when he met the most important person in the worst nightmare he could imagine.....my dad. For sure, God has a good sense of humor.

3. **Listen to a Wise Mother's Counsel**—No one loves their children like a good mother. Fathers love and protect in a different way than mothers. Mothers who stay in touch with God through prayer and reading God's Word can be confident in their counsel sessions...especially with their children. Dad sincerely grieved over the ordeal with Don. He was the one that had to break the bad news to the family. He was the one that wept and turned inward for over 4 days trying to sort out the mess that he found his family in. Not until he witnessed his daughter releasing her pain to the Almighty and forgiving her daddy for bringing that painful moment into her life, was he willing to forgive himself. Mom, on the other hand, knew that the reality of finding out the truth was a "God Thing." Her counsel with her daughter was crucial to this scene that ended in victory for the Cumby family. My mom was the Margaret Thatcher of our little clan. She was gracious, wise, brave, and humble. She was a person with a pure heart...a real "Peace Maker." "Blessed are the pure in heart, for they

will see God. Blessed are the peacemakers, for they will be called the sons/daughters of God…" (Matthew 5:8-9).

4. **"…You may be sure that your sin will find you out" (Numbers 32:23).** What more needs to be said?

There are so many different chasms and treacherous terrains on the road in which we travel every day, we must depend on all of the gems of truth the "bridge builders" have engrained in us to keep us balanced and ready for all the uneven occurrences in our life. It is ironic, of course, to know that God has placed specific people in our lives to grow us and direct us toward the mark of the high calling of God. Never do we have to worry about whether we will have problems and trials in this life; what we should be concerned about is how we are to respond to those "bumps in the road." Will we lose control? Will we put on the brakes when we need to accelerate? Will we refuse to go when He tells us to move? Will we refuse to stop when He tells us to wait? In it all, will we say to the Lord, "I will go where you want me to go, dear Lord" or will we refuse to take a step forward in order to get passed life's critical challenges?

My dad and mom built bridges over those challenging chasms of life. My sister and my brothers all knew that we inherited great treasures from our parents. "Money"….we did not receive! "Honey"...from the Rock...we did....in abundance.

Scripture:

"...with honey from the rock I (the Lord) would satisfy you" (Psalm 81:16b).

"Eat honey, my son, for it is good; honey from the comb is sweet to your taste. Know also that wisdom is sweet to your soul; if you find it, there is a future hope for you,...." (Proverbs 24:13-14a).

Gerald E. Cumby

Hymn for Spiritual Nourishment:

When upon life's billows you are tempest tossed,
When you are discouraged, thinking all is lost,
Count your many blessings, name them one by one,
And it will surprise you what the Lord has done.

Are you ever burdened with a load of care?
Does the cross seem heavy you are called to bear?
Count your many blessings, every doubt will fly,
And you will be singing as the days go by.

When you look at others with their lands and gold,
Think that Christ has promised you His wealth untold;
Count your many blessings, money cannot buy
Your reward in heaven, nor your home on high.

So, amid the conflict, whether great or small,
Do not be discouraged, God is over all;
Count your many blessings, angels will attend,
Help and comfort give you to your journey's end.

Chorus:
Count your many blessings, name them one by one;
Count your blessings, see what God hath done;

Text by: Johnson Oatman, Jr.

Chapter 11

Building Confidence

"Listen, my sons, to a father's instruction; pay attention and gain understanding. I give you sound learning, so do not forsake my teaching. When I was a boy in my father's house, still tender, and an only child of my mother, he taught me and said, 'Lay hold of my words with all your heart; keep my commands and you will live. Get wisdom, get understanding; do not forget my words or swerve from them. Do not forsake wisdom, and she will protect you; love her, and she will watch over you. Wisdom is supreme; therefore get wisdom. Though it cost all you have, get understanding. Esteem her, and she will exalt you; embrace her, and she will honor you. She will set a garland of grace on your head and present you with a crown of splendor"
(Proverbs 4:1-9).
"For <u>the Lord will be your confidence</u> and will keep your foot from being snared" (Proverbs 3:26).

I was a very inquisitive young whipper-snapper (so my grandpa would say). I wanted to know why the water in the creek ran one way and not the other, why some animals had long tails and others did not, why ants were ever created by God, and why horny toads looked so mean, etc. I would get into trouble by asking too many questions as to where I came from, how my little brothers came along and why......why girls played "jacks" and I should not, etc. Incidentally, I did play "jacks" and I think every one should play this wonderful hand-to-eye game to help with coordination and instill competition across gender lines (no kidding).

Back to my train of thought as to me being inquisitive about life and other important things, let me trudge on. I wanted to do what my big brothers did. I wanted to ride a bicycle while others my age were riding tricycles, and I wanted to wear boots instead of tennis shoes. However, when I found out I could run faster with tennis shoes than boots, I changed my mind. I caused Mom and Dad to think, "What in the world are we going to do when this boy grows up?"

I was 5 years old and had not started to school. We were living in Stephenville, Texas while Dad was building bridges on one of the major state highways in the area. Our residence was a rented house in the country on the outskirts of town. There were several acres of land around the house where we lived. A stock tank was on the property about ¼ mile from our home. A holding tank located right outside our back door provided water for the family. The holding tank (a 500 gallon tank) was about 15' above the ground on wooden legs. Water was received in the house by pressure flowing down to the kitchen and one bathtub.

One of my adventures and major challenges included learning to ride my brother's bicycle. The bicycle was much too much of a "big kid's" bike than what I should learn to ride. The handlebars were over my head (a girl's bike without the middle bar), and I was not large enough to control my destination. If Doyle, my brother who was 6 years older, was running next to me, I was confident enough to get on the bike and ride it. When I started to fall, Doyle would catch me and hold the bike up before it fell to the side.

Doyle did not mind me riding the bike....so long as he was running along beside me. He specifically told me not to try to ride the bicycle while he was at school. The temptation was too much for me, however, because I wanted to ride when I wanted to ride.

While Doyle was at school, I got on the bicycle and tried to ride down the road from my home going toward the mail box (about ¼ mile). This was, of course, a major mistake. Not only did I fall from the bicycle, but I also damaged the tire and fender of the bicycle. I was in trouble and I knew it. The skinned knee and elbow let me know that I had a "boo-boo" that could not be covered up. The damage to the bike also had a "boo-boo" that could not be covered up. I was going to be in "big trouble" with mama....and my brother Doyle.

I left the bike in the middle of the road (I couldn't push it up the hill) and ran back to the house to find a place to hide. I hid behind an old icebox, in the corner next to an old storage closet.

It was only 30 minutes before Doyle came home, and Mom had already started to look for me by the time Doyle made it to the house. Doyle found the bicycle as he was walking up the road when he came home from school. The two started to search for me with diligence for the next hour. My sister (Pat) and older brother

(Joe) came home from school and all of them started to look for me as the afternoon was beginning to fade away.

After two hours of searching in the house and out near the barns, fields, and even down near the stock tank, all of them started to cry and think the worst. Mom was nearly hysterical and the brothers and sister were having a major crying spell. I was now at the point of enjoying hearing my brothers' cry. I had never been the object of such concern before (that I could remember). I was "the man of the hour" and every body was going to really love me when I would make my grand appearance to show them that nothing tragic had happened. I heard Mom say in a very shrill voice, "Here comes Dad and I can't stand to tell him. Dear God, help us."

I could see the whole scene played out from a window beside the old storage closet. Dad jumped out of his pickup seeing that something was dreadfully wrong. The kids were crying and Mom could not even tell Daddy without weeping about my disappearance. My whole family was weeping over "little old me."

I saw Dad wilt when he received the news. They told him where they had looked for me and Dad asked if they had looked in the water storage tank. He had told me on one other occasion to not ever climb up on the ladder to look in the storage tank. Knowing my inquisitive spirit, Dad started to climb the ladder. I could see that he was shaking and had tears in his eyes. Therefore, I felt that it might be wise to make my appearance. If my hiding went on past this particular time, I thought that my mother and father would have a heart attack.

I came out from behind the icebox, opened the back door, held out my arms and said, "Here I am, I'm not lost." My mom and siblings all ran to me and wept for joy. They were hugging and kissing me. Mom just wilted with emotion as she held me close to her.

All the time they were showing their affection for me, I had one eye on them and one eye on my dad. Dad started to climb back down off the ladder. His countenance changed from a concerned and grieving parent mode to a fearful, but stern, look as he walked toward me. I peeled myself from mom, held out my arms, and said, "Hi, Dad, here I am!" Dad replied, "Hi, Gerald; and son, I am going to bust your rear-end".....and....he did. Mom was trying to love me and Dad was popping my behind.

Most of the time Mom and Dad were on the same page with discipline. Mom did not question Dad's handling of discipline matters. Dad was so mad at me that he reacted in fury....but love at the same time. He knew that I knew what I did. He knew that I did it with a selfish and unrepentant heart. He knew that I was not thinking about what the consequences for my mom, my siblings, and my father were.

The consequences of this awful experience taught me a lesson that could not be said in a word of encouragement, discouragement, or wise counsel. I look back on it now and I saw that Dad was not doing what Dr. Spock suggested in all the books on discipline; but, he did what was needed for me at the time. He did for me what no one else could or would do. He made a statement to me that has stuck with me to this day.....

"You don't hurt your family by your stubbornness and selfishness."

If parents, spouses, children, and other family members would consider the deep and devastating hurt experienced in divorce, drug use, alcohol use, and rebellion in general before they get involved in such measures, they would not take the next step to breaking hearts and family ties. I know that this experience with my dad was a major break-through in my young life. I remembered it when I was 6....at 36....56....and to this day.

What can you learn from my experience? Will you question my dad's discipline measures? Will you tell your kids that they would never have to worry about being spanked for their acts of rebellion and selfishness? I hope not. My dad did not have to use such measures very many times in my life. In every case in which I received "corporal punishment" I deserved it. My self-esteem was not crushed and my "little mind" was not placed in a holding pattern. The only thing in my little selfish world that was hurt was my back-side (and that was for a short time).

Yes, this type of counsel and parental discipline might not be "politically correct" and not approved by the Child Welfare Office. It was, however, the best counsel and means for maturing the wayfaring child that I know.

Now you know a little more about the "Bridge Builder" in my family. Dad had a heart of love for his family; however, he used and defined "tough love" before James Dobson ever thought about it. Please, this is no criticism of Mr. Dobson. I love his work and his methods for discipline and maturing of the family. He is one of my favorite writers and I would have loved to have him counsel me as I was growing up (maybe even after I grew up and had children of my own). In fact, I read his work now and I say, "Yes" and "Amen" to his style and commitment of walking families through family crisis. He is truly a great man of "the Word" and a man of his word.

"Endure hardship as discipline; God is treating you as sons. For what son is not disciplined by his father? If you are not disciplined (and everyone undergoes discipline), then you are illegitimate children and not true sons. Moreover, we have all had human fathers who disciplined us and we respected them for it. How much more should we submit to the Father of our spirits and live! Our fathers disciplined us for a little while as they thought best; but God disciplines us for our good, that we may share in His holiness. No discipline seems pleasant at the time, but painful. Later on, however, it produces a harvest of righteousness and peace for those who have been trained by it" (Hebrews 12:7-11).

Hymn of Confidence:

How firm a foundation, ye saints of the Lord,
Is laid for your faith in His excellent Word!
What more can He say than to you He hath said,
To you who for refuge to Jesus have fled?

Fear not, I am with thee; O be not dismayed,
For I am thy God, and will still give thee aid;
I'll strengthen thee, help thee, and cause thee to stand,
Upheld by My righteous, omnipotent hand.

When through fiery trials thy pathway shall lie,
My grace, all sufficient, shall be thy supply:
The flame shall not hurt thee; I only design
Thy dross to consume and thy gold to refine.

The soul that on Jesus hath leaned for repose
I will not, I will not desert to its foes;
That soul, though all hell should endeavor to shake,
I'll never, no, never, no, never forsake!"

Rippon's Selection of Hymns, 1787

Chapter 12

Character Building

"Children, obey your parents in the Lord, for this right. Honor your father and mother—which is the first commandment with a promise—that it may go well with you and that you may enjoy long life on earth" (Ephesians 6:1-3).

I don't know of too many students who have been suspended from school for fighting. I have heard other teachers tell of some "wayward kids" who have gotten into disputes at school and would take their licks and give some out in trying to prove one being right over another. Peer pressure or quick tempers were usually the reasons for punching first and thinking last. However, every once in a while one would hear of an admirable fight that might have been observed when someone would take up for what was right and there would be another that would feel the same way about his or her position.

Although I don't condone the idea of fist-fighting for a good cause (my grandkids might say different), there are times when a kid, or an adult, just can't stand it any more and just have to swing instead of wisely backing out of a situation. Hand-to-hand battles or physical fighting have been going on since sin was defined and good intentions were defied.

As to suspensions from school, usually we find this type action taking place at the Junior High (Middle School) or Senior High School level. However, let me explain how I was suspended from the public schools in the first week I attended the first grade at Stephenville, Texas. How this was going to get around to character building only God knew at the time. How this is going to be explained in this book and still be part of Bridge Building for God's Kingdom is going to be recognized only when the story is told and the Holy Spirit provides the proper insight to the readers of this book. God's infinite wisdom is not always recognized instantly or after a few days of rewinding the clock and restructuring our thoughts as to why this or that happened. Maybe you will recognize God's hand in this true story of a dumb and unwise decision by a dad of 38 and a young lad barely 6 years old.

Dad, like any father, wanted his sons to mature into wise, handsome, and godly young men. Maybe not in that order, but those were the three traits Dad was striving to instill into his sons as he led them through life. His gifts to us, however, did not always reflect that of a wise father. Candy at the grocery store on Saturday night, Nu-Grape soda pop, peanuts and/or Popcorn were the treats Dad would have in mind when he went with Mom to the store every Saturday night. I think that he felt he owed it to us for being out of town so much. I think back on it now and know that we really did not need this kind of "stuff" that Dad was buying for us at the store. Mom would have for us every day a cake, pie and/or baked pie crust that would be left over from her baking for the day. We did not go hungry at the Cumby household. We didn't have much; but, we were well-fed and happy.

Every dad seemed to want their son or sons to be hunters or defenders of the household during my childhood. I don't ever remember Dad begging me or encouraging me to join the local Little League or Pee-Wee Football Teams in the area where we were located (I don't even know if they had Pee-Wee Football back in my childhood days).

For my 6th birthday present, however, my dad bought me something that I will never forget. It was a knife (a small, straight shaft knife with a scabbard). I can picture that knife now. It had a blade on it that was shiny, pointed and very sharp. I could attach the scabbard to my belt and place the knife straight down into it and then secure it with a snap to hold the knife in place.

Dad gave me this knife with some directions (not written, but verbal). The directions came after my Mom had burned my dad pretty good for buying me the weapon in the first place. Dad recoiled like a cat running up against a dog.... and defended himself by saying, "Yes, honey, I will make sure Gerald knows that he is not to do anything with the knife accept to:

1. Use when defending the Fort (Home)
2. Use when defending against the tigers and mountain lions in the area (We never saw Tigers and Mountain Lions around the house)

3. Use when attacking snakes that might sneak up
    on my mom (laughing when saying it).

<u>And (seriously speaking now), to use only in time of
an emergency when all other methods of defense have
failed. Last, but not least, never carry the knife away from
the house unless Dad or an older brother was with me.</u>

Did I understand anything Dad told me? Of course
I did......about like I understood Calculus or Trigonom-
etry at the ripe old age of six. All I know....I had a knife
that was mine and it was going to defend me from anyone invading my territory.

May I again remind the reader that I was still the
rambunctious and "never still" young boy that had
brought the fear of God into my family by hiding for
long periods of time trying to get my way and delaying
the discipline that was sure to come my way.

My first day of school (1st grade, no available kinder-
garten back then) found me excited and ready to tell
the teacher that 2 plus 2 was four and that I could ride
a bicycle. My excitement ended when the teacher told
me to be seated and make sure that I did not bother
other students. I listened and I could not believe that
we were going to have to be quiet for at least 30 minutes.

Recess came and I found myself trying to make
friends. I was barely 6 and thought I was a teen-ager.
What I did not know and understand is that there was
another little boy that thought he was king on the
mountain, too. He had the girls swooning and the boys
backing up and giving him the ground that he was stating that he owned. He made sure everybody on the

playground knew that he was the person in charge of the swings, the slides, and the merry-go-round.

The girls were afraid that he was going to hurt them because he wanted to swing them too high and make the merry-go-round go too fast. The boys stepped back and let him swing those few girls that were brave enough to let him swing them. One of the girls fell out of the swing and the teacher ran over and asked how it happened. Everybody was afraid of Tommy (the bully) and would not tell the teacher anything; even the little girl that was hurt was afraid to tell the teacher.

Tommy was in charge of the playground and the school cafeteria. He would drink the milk of those kids that were afraid not to give it to him. I did not like school after the first day; and, I sure did not like Tommy.

Basically, the same thing happened the next day. The teachers were getting a little wiser as to how Tommy was always involved in every little fracas that took place. They warned him that he was to keep his hands to himself and his mouth shut. This made Tommy even more determined to be Mr. Big on Campus and maintain his territory on the playground.

By the third day, I had just about enough of Tommy and I was determined to take care of the issue. Tommy was about 20 pounds heavier than all the 1st graders (accept Myrtle, she was the largest little girl I had ever seen). Myrtle was eating everything Tommy was not eating. She really wasn't a fighter…but, boy, could she eat!

I knew that if I fought Tommy I would go home with a black eye or worse. This would get me in trouble anyway (Dad and Mom would know I had been fighting if

I came home scratched, bruised or my clothes torn). Therefore, if I'm going to be in trouble one way or the other, I might as well make sure Tommy doesn't continue to make my life miserable. I don't remember if I even thought about all the other miserable souls that had feared Tommy's wrath, but my world could not afford Tommy's bullying every day at school. I wanted my share of the swing set, my share of the slide, and I wanted to ride the merry-go-round at a speed that I wanted it to go. I also wanted my milk and did not want Tommy to invade my territory.

Disobeying my daddy's rules, I took my knife to school. I hid it under my shirt until recess and, when Tommy pushed everybody out of the way while he slid down the slide, I met him at the bottom of the slide next to a large tree on the school playground. I pinned him up against the tree and had the knife against his nose. I don't remember the exact words I used, but it was something like, "You little smart-alec, I am fixing to cut you, skin you, and place your skin on the chalk board for every one to see." (Boy....that was a real manly and godly thing to say). I think I also finished the conversation, "Do you understand that....hoss?"

Tommy screamed like a monkey being chased by a tiger. The teachers were on me before Tommy could get his second breath. I told the teacher that the "little punk was not going to drink my milk and keep all the other kids off the swings."

They were not impressed with my reasoning or my actions. They had me in the principal's office before I could tell them my name and address. I was paddled and given some very distinct instructions as to what was in store for me for the next few days. I was suspended before I knew what suspended meant.

The principal took me home because Mom did not drive and Dad had the pickup at work. Mom was so embarrassed for my actions and cried all the rest of the day until Dad came home. Dad cried a lot, too. He took my knife away and I never was given a knife by my dad or siblings for the rest of my life.

Dad and Mom discussed the issue with each other that evening. I know that Mom stated several times to Dad that he ought to be punished along with me over this incident. She did not want me to get out of the discipline that was coming to me. She felt that Dad needed to handle it the way that he knew he ought to handle it.

Dad spoke to me with the strongest discipline that I have ever had in my life. He did not scream, but he let me know how disappointed he was for my disobedience, for my lack of wisdom, for my disregard of every thing that we had ever been taught concerning character and integrity and why I was a "Cumby." He said the Cumby name in the school system had been destroyed and dishonored.

I never will forget the look on Dad's face as he was taking the knife away from me. He was crying, but he was furious as he broke the knife at the handle. He placed the broken knife in the scabbard and I never saw the knife again. I then bent over as instructed and Dad gave me several licks with his belt. I cried a lot that week and the week-end that followed.

It was quiet around the house for the next week. I do remember, however, that I was not allowed to go back to school for the next few days. Mom told me later in life that I then received counseling from several people at school before I was allowed back in class. My Mother and Dad were also counseled to make sure that they understood the consequences of my actions.

I know that many of you who are reading this story are wondering what ever happened to Tommy. Tommy was also sent home the day of the incident, but came back the next day. I never had any more trouble with him while we were at Stephenville.

Of course, when I was allowed back in class after the incident at Stephenville, I never had any friends. At least that is what I remember. I sat in the corner of the 1st grade teacher's room and no kid was supposed to turn around and look at me. I did receive one note that I can remember after we learned our ABCs and could write a complete sentence. One of the little girls (not Myrtle) passed me a note when I was going to the lunch room and said that I could "have her milk that day....and tanks." I did not know what she meant by "tanks" until it occurred to me that she misspelled "thanks."

Dad finished his job of building the bridges around Stephenville a few months later and we moved to Abilene where I completed the first grade.

Hopefully, Tommy turned out to be a fine man that loved God, Country, and his fellow man. I pray that my actions did not do anything that would harm Tommy or anyone involved in the incident. I do know without a shadow of doubt that it hurt two of the finest people that I have ever known....my mom and my dad.

What have I gained from this experience in my young life? I think if I did not keep reminding myself of the incident and asking Mom for her opinion and knowledge as to what really went on during this time, I would have probably forgotten about it.

I have told this story to my children and grandchildren (and a few others). I have received some laughs from some...and I have received some severe criticism from others. I think the criticism from many adults (even some children) have been against my parents. Of course, I don't appreciate the verbal criticism against my parents. Many say that it would not have happened had Dad not bought the knife for me at such an early age. Many say that Mom should have insisted that Dad take the knife away from me when I received it and saved it for a future date to give to me when I became more responsible.

To summarize and give final conclusion to this story, I know that the real culprit was me. Just because I was given a gift by my father, I did not use the gift correctly, nor did I use wise counsel from previous lectures from Dad. I was not to use the knife outside the boundaries in which I was emphatically instructed. I disobeyed. The guilty party was me and my foolishness brought a tainted scar on my family name.

Where can we see the character building traits of this chapter? First, let us understand what character means. At least it is what I want it to mean to me and to the reader.

Your character is normally defined by what you do, not necessarily what you say or believe. I feel that good character requires doing the right thing, even when it is costly or risky. The result or "pay off" for having good character is that it makes you a better person and it makes the world around you a better place.

One of the six traits of good character is trustworthiness. I had to learn trustworthiness from my dad and mom. I feel that this is one of the missing links in today's society. Hearing of the failure of marriages, of young people dropping out of school, teachers not being trusted with our young children and teen-agers, preachers and priests being irresponsible with funds or give reason to believe that they have violated the confidence necessary in working with our spouses, children, etc. cause us to not to trust the system of which is so broken today.

The system I am referring to is not tied to a particular era, a particular facet of life known only in America, or a single area that can be pinpointed as susceptible for change. The system is what has been in effect since Adam and Eve had to leave the Garden of Eden due to their disobedience of a simple rule that was initiated and required by a Holy God at the time. That rule is still in effect today; rule #1, obey. Not obeying brings a curse and obeying brings blessing.

The system is really black and white; a choice between good and evil. I know that this may cause many people reading this book to stop and refrain from reading the rest of the chapters...or maybe for the sake of being inquisitive, keep reading and try to understand what is meant here.

The answer to life's simplest of questions from many philosophers and, even preachers, is "it depends" (gray area thinking). I simply declare that the theory of relativity is just that, a theory. It is a misnomer and inappropriate. I realize that there are some things that we don't want a "yes" or "no" answer. We want either something in between or something that would be temporarily satisfying. The truth is sometimes hard to swallow. Satisfaction is in the eye and the mind of the beholder and the idea of compromise makes life seem simple and easier to grasp.

The truth in my case, I made the wrong choice and disobeyed my earthly father. I, in turn, caused great distress for my father and mother and the Cumby name. Have I made amends? Have I made up for my misgivings? Have I been forgiven for my sin that you would think after reading this chapter is "ever before me?" Praise God, I have been forgiven and that blight that was on our name has been stricken from the pages of history at Stephenville Public Schools.

I know you are saying, "That was in the records of your school activities at Stephenville?" The answer is, "Probably not!" However, in my book of memory, it was there. I caused pain for many people and the pain was a "thorn in my side for years." Dad never mentioned any part of the situation after we left Stephenville. However, in my mind he questioned my trustworthiness for several years after the incident.

The other character traits that I learned from this early experience in life were respect, responsibility, fairness, and caring. If you go back and see all the details of this chapter and the story of the suspended first grader, you will see where there is one or more of these character traits exemplified in my dad and mom. They cared for my future. They were fair in their dealing with me and my problem. They made me responsible for my disobedience; although they gained some great wisdom here from dealing with the responsible party. They respected the school for dealing with the situation and I learned to respect my parents as to why I must obey.

The most important teaching and main concept gained from this experience is that my family is the most important part of growing up....and living up to the name and what it means to the community is all a part of it. God and country are vital entities that help us understand respect and trustworthiness, but it is instilled in us by the family that we inherited.

To go further, what we as Christians say and do either enhances or diminishes the Christian name and the furtherance of the gospel of Jesus Christ.

Two of the most famous quotes on trustworthiness are found in the words of George Washington and Abraham Lincoln. Washington stated, "*I hope I shall always possess firmness and virtue enough to maintain what I consider the most enviable of all titles, the character of an honest man.*" Abraham Lincoln said, "*No man has a good enough memory to make a successful liar.*" I find that both quotes are worthy to remember and to heed as we progress down the road of life.

As one of my senior mentors in life stated, "Some people can be taught; others have to be learned." That "learned" part is the hardest. It may not be good English, but it gets the point over.

"Honesty is the first chapter in the book of wisdom."
~ Thomas Jefferson

"Honesty is the best policy. If I lose mine honor, I lose myself." ~ William Shakespeare

"A liar will not be believed, even when he speaks the truth." ~ Aesop

"I have found that being honest is the best technique I can use. Right up front, tell people what you're trying to accomplish and what you're willing to sacrifice to accomplish it." ~ Lee Iacocca

"It only takes one lie to taint your entire testimony in a court of law. Honesty is a vital part of having a good reputation." ~ Jim Rohn

"Who lies for you will lie against you." ~ Bosnian Proverb

"Oh, what a tangled web we weave, When first we practice to deceive!" ~ Sir Walter Scott

"No matter how brilliant a man may be, he will never engender confidence in his subordinates and associates if he lacks simple honesty and moral courage." ~ J. Lawton Collins

"Rather than love, than money, than fame, give me truth." ~ *Thoreau*

"In a time of universal deceit, telling the truth is a revolutionary act." ~ *George Orwell*

"When a well-packaged web of lies has been sold gradually to the masses over generations, the truth will seem utterly preposterous and its speaker a raving lunatic." ~ *Dresden James*

The elite of our government officials need to always remember the following quote below from Robert Green Ingersoll. I never desire that we in America uphold to the fact that everyone should be on equal terms as to wealth, or that the least responsible job deserves the same pay as the most responsible one. However, the quote deserves a look, as well as a promise not to forget.

"There is something wrong in a government where they who do the most have the least. There is something wrong when honesty wears a rag, and rascality a robe; when the loving, the tender, eat a crust, while the infamous sit at banquets." ~ *Robert Green Ingersoll*

Honesty and truthfulness are rare treasures in today's day and age. As these famous quotes above clearly indicate, holding on to the truth and clothing ourselves in honesty are the only way we can do our part to repair the portions of this world that lies have begun to eat away.

Note: The previous quotes were found in:
16 Famous Quotes to Celebrate Honesty Day
Posted: Thursday, April 19, 2007 by Noel Jameson
http://www.famous-quotes-and-quotations.com

Genesis 18:19

For I have chosen him, so that he will direct his children and his household after him to keep the way of the LORD by doing what is right and just, so that the LORD will bring about for Abraham what he has promised him.

Exodus 18:21

But select capable men from all the people—men who fear God, trustworthy men who hate dishonest gain—

Psalm 15

LORD, who may dwell in your sanctuary? Who may live on your holy hill? He whose walk is blameless and who does what is righteous, who speaks the truth from his heart and has no slander on his tongue, who does his neighbor no wrong and casts no slur on his fellowman, who despises a vile man but honors those who fear the LORD, who keeps his oath even when it hurts, who lends his money without usury and does not accept a bribe against the innocent. He who does these things will never be shaken.

Proverbs 4:23-27

Above all else, guard your heart, for it is the wellspring of life. Put away perversity from your mouth; keep corrupt talk far from your lips. Let your eyes look straight ahead, fix your gaze directly before you. Make level paths for your feet and take only ways that are firm. Do not swerve to the right or the left; keep your foot from evil.

Hymn of Dedication and A Call For Integrity:

Have thine own way, Lord! Have thine own way!
Thou art the potter, I am the clay.
Mold me and make me after thy will,
while I am waiting, yielded and still.

Have thine own way, Lord! Have thine own way!
Search me and try me, Savior today!
Wash me just now, Lord, wash me just now,
as in thy presence humbly I bow.

Have thine own way, Lord! Have thine own way!
Wounded and weary, help me I pray!
Power, all power, surely is thine!
Touch me and heal me, Savior divine!

Have thine own way, Lord! Have thine own way!
Hold o'er my being absolute sway.
Fill with thy Spirit till all shall see
Christ only, always, living in me!

Text: Adelaide A. Pollard, 1862-1934

Chapter 13

Building The Bridge Across The Generation Gap

"Remember your leaders, who spoke the Word of God to you. Consider the outcome of their way of life and imitate their faith" *(Hebrews 13:7).*

"Leaders are not born, they are made." This is a memorable quote and a great inspirational thought; however, it is not biblical or necessarily true. The Word of God states, "the word of the Lord came to me, saying, 'before I formed you in the womb I knew you, before you were born I set you apart; I appointed you as a prophet to the nations" (Jeremiah 1:4-5). That is biblical and therefore a truth. Therefore, if God intended for me to be a leader and His purpose is for me to be a leader, He will provide avenues and directions for me to accomplish His goal. However, if I choose to disallow His intentions by wrong choices and rebellious actions, He will allow me to get off the path of the purpose He has intended for me. He will allow it only because He will not force us to obey. Obedience must be a willful choice.

God has a purpose and plan for our lives (Jeremiah 29:11) and He is a God that is not partial to one over another, "for the Lord your God is God of gods and

Lord of lords, the great God, mighty and awesome, who shows no partiality and accepts no bribes" (Deuteronomy 10:17). I believe and strongly promote this truth. I don't try to understand or challenge God on any statement from His Word. Therefore, if it is not in His purpose or plan for me to be a leader, then He plans for me to be the best follower I can be. Every leader needs purposeful followers and every follower needs a leader who provides the best alternative for accomplishing set purposes and goals. Paul said, "I press on toward the goal to win the prize for which God has called me heavenward in Christ Jesus" (Philippians 3:14). That is our goal and, whether we are a follower or a leader, we must press on to win the prize God has called us.

I have found that there are many leaders that have a hard time learning to be a follower. To be the leader God has called us, we must learn to follow His directions for our lives and to humble ourselves in order to have a positive relationship with Him. Followers have always desired to have someone lead them. It is easier for the follower to yield to the Masters calling. Although followers can be led astray (i.e., Jim Jones tragedy), the follower has a much more tender heart when it comes to giving in to the calling and direction of God by the Holy Spirit than the leader who still has an arrogant spirit living within. Paul said, "Are you so foolish? After beginning with the Spirit, <u>are you now trying to attain your goal by human effort?</u>" (Galatians 3:3).

My dad was a leader. God blessed him by giving him skills that helped him lead others in the right direction. He, like any man, had his faults. At times, quick tempered, but usually because of wrongs done to man by man. He could not stand to be in the presence of a liar and one who was lazy and shunned responsibilities. His temper would flare up when he saw someone mistreat a less fortunate person. He had no patience with anyone who was arrogant or promiscuous. He could not hold his tongue when someone was verbally mistreating a spouse, child, or one who was trying to serve others. Also, his temper really flared when someone he knew was married and was flirting with waitresses or other "cute things" in the restaurants and hotels he patronized.

I was quite aware of an incident in which my father was involved with a State Bridge Inspector that he knew that was in the same restaurant he had frequented. Mom and I were with dad at a table next to the inspector when the inspector became engaged in a conversation with a young waitress that was well endowed by the Creator of all people and all things.

Since God is no respecter of persons and certainly not a partial God, this lady might have proved Him wrong (but I won't question that because God does not lie). I suppose what God gives to one person and doesn't another, He will make up for it either in intelligence or other positive physical features.

Anyway, the inspector was asking the waitress all kind of questions that was leading to a promiscuous meeting later that night. With me sitting next to Mom, I overheard a very unbecoming word from the inspector's mouth that triggered a physical reaction from me. It triggered Dad's physical and spiritual emotions, also.

Dad stood up, turned around to the inspector, and told him, "Hey 'hoss", if you do not refrain from such speech coming from your filthy mouth, I am going to shut it for you." The inspector was stunned to see dad's reaction. Dad went on to tell the waitress that this man was married and was about the sorriest specimen of a human being that he knew.

Mom was trying to get my dad to sit back down. The waitress immediately moved from the table leaving Dad staring in the eyes of the inspector that would be on his job the next morning. The inspector apologized to my dad and our family. He left the table and Dad sat down and ate his meal.

The waitress suddenly became the best waitress we have seen in a long time. She asked us if we wanted more tea at least ten times.

Dad said that the inspector did not show up for work the next morning. The state sent another inspector out to Dad's job and he was there until the project was completed on the bridge and culvert work in the area.

Could Dad have handled this incident differently? Probably; but, I liked the way he handled it. Yes, he could have taken the "compassionate and less controversial" way out and simply gone over to the inspector and whispered in his ear, "You are married, and your conversation is not becoming to you." He could have said, "Hey, Jack, let's keep the bad language down and you need to remember that you need to call your wife!" And, of course, Dad could have looked at Mom and me and stated in a whispered voice, "This is not our business, and we will let God handle it."

All of the "probablies" in the previous paragraph as to how to handle the particular situation would be wrong in my way of thinking. I don't like compromise and I don't like handing God a problem that He certainly can handle, but is expecting us to be the one to do His business. Responses such as "I'll pray about it" or, "we don't need to get involved in an affair that is not our business" are "cop outs" and have serious consequences both here on earth and when we stand before God at our heavenly hearing. I certainly believe in prayer and I know that God loves His children to call on Him for help, but we need to put our feet to action and not stand in the corner praying and waiting for God to do our job for us.

What did I learn from this? A bunch! Standing for truth, doing what is right, speaking up against wrong, hating arrogance and pride, and calling a sin…. "sin"… is in my physical, emotional, and spiritual make-up. Taking this trait from my dad, I have tried to follow in his footsteps. Yes, I have opened my mouth before engaging my brain. Yes, I have strongly replied when I should let a conversation die. And, yes…I have later questioned myself in hindsight upon responding to unjust or questionable situations. However, I have not compromised my principles or my values, even if my responses were not "politically correct."

This trait of standing up for what I believe is Biblical and true without compromise has been rewarding at times; and, I do know that it will be most rewarding when I stand before God. I can say, however, that my actions in standing up for what I know to be right have cost me monetarily and in receiving promotions in my profession (management).

I have always believed that "you can win and still lose....and you can lose and still win." Winning a promotion, receiving bonuses and substantial raises sometime requires the compromising of personal values and principles. That is a win...but involves a tragic loss. By standing my ground as to what I believe to be true and in line with God's principles has caused me to lose a significant promotion where there would have been a lucrative pay increase that would have amounted to at least $65,000 over a 5 year period. However, $65,000 would not have started to pay my hospital bills and sleepless nights if I had given in to "political correctness" in the business world at the time.

Hopefully, the experience above does not cause you to feel sorry for me or cause you to think that I want to bring to light any wrong that was committed against me. Nothing could be further from the truth. The failure to receive the promotion and the extra monetary benefits has been a blessing and a wonderful experience leading to a much richer and fuller life with family and friends. This experience was one of many that have proved that "God has a plan for our lives" and when we yield to His leading, we will be winners no matter where we go, what He has us to do, or who we meet and greet on the way to our destination.

My dad's personal character traits have certainly been engrained in my spirit and personal life. As I find myself walking in my father's shoes, I want my children (who are grown and have children of their own) to have a desire to walk in their father's and mother's shoes when it comes to standing up for truth and what is right according to the Word of God. I see that trait in them as they go through life. They have certainly blessed their mom and dad as they are holding on to those character traits that they saw in us as the challenges and struggles in our lives were being experienced and solutions were being resolved.

We were not perfect parents. We know that to be a true statement better than anyone else. There are little reminders of our struggles and issues in life that were not always handled appropriately. It is our desire, however, that our grown children will "arise and call her (their mother) blessed" and that they have "listened to their father and mother, who gave them life." I know that my children have the utmost respect for their mom and dad. We appreciate the fact that they have brought their children (our grandchildren) up in the ways of the Lord.

As I listen to our daughters communicate and handle situations in life (married 28 years and 26 years respectively...to the same spouses), I am proud of their walk... their talk...and their respect for the Word of God. They are, with full support of their husbands, standing on the foundation of truth in which they were raised. Not only that, they are handing down to their children those traits established as they were growing up in our home. Prayerfully, we give our daughters, our sons-in-law, and our grandchildren into the Lord's hands. Every morning my wife and I pray for their protection and safety. We do, however, put those prayers into action by letting them know that we expect them to stay on the right path where the Lord can honor our prayers. Sounds a little presumptuous, but we would rather nudge our children than try to nudge the Lord. With all respect to our Mighty God, we know that His plans for our lives are for the best. We do, however, know that He will not give us what we desire unless it brings glory to Him.

Passing down to our offspring the blessings of God is what it is all about for our family. That is why our whole family prays, plays, gives and lives with hearts united.

"Blessed is he whose transgressions are forgiven, whose sins are covered. Blessed is the man whose sin the Lord does not count against him, and whose spirit is no deceit" (Psalm 32:1-2).

"You are my hiding place; you will protect me from trouble and surround me with songs of deliverance. I will instruct you and teach you in the way you should go; I will counsel you and watch over you. Do not be like the horse or the mule, which have no understanding but must be controlled by bit and bridle or they will not come to you. Many are the woes of the wicked, but the Lord's unfailing love surrounds the man who trusts in him" (Psalm 32:7-10).

Hymn about Him (Jesus):

Tell me the story of Jesus, write on my heart every word;
Tell me the story most precious, sweetest that ever
was heard. Tell how the angels in chorus...sang as
they welcomed His birth, "Glory to God in the highest! Peace and good tidings to earth."

Tell me the story of Jesus, write on my heart every word;
Tell me the story most precious, sweetest that ever
was heard.

Tell of the cross where they nailed Him, writhing in
anguish and pain; Tell of the grave where they laid
Him, Tell how He liveth again. Love in that story
so tender, clearer than ever I see: Stay, let me weep
while you whisper, Love paid the ransom for me.

Tell me the story of Jesus, write on my heart every word;
Tell me the story most precious, sweetest that ever
was heard.

By Fanny J. Crosby.

Chapter 14

The Bridge To Shaping Godly Work Ethics

"Be careful not to do your 'acts of righteousness' before men, to be seen by them. If you do, you will have no reward from your Father in heaven. So when you give to the needy, do not announce it with trumpets, as the hypocrites do in the synagogues and on the streets, to be honored by men. I tell you the truth; they have received their reward in full. But when you give to the needy, do not let your left hand know what your right hand is doing, so that your giving may be in secret. Then your Father, who sees what is done in secret, will reward you" (Matthew 6:1-4).

"They did not require an accounting from those to whom they gave the money to pay the workers, because they acted with complete honesty" (2 Kings 12:15).

"Dishonest money dwindles away, but he who gathers money little by little makes it grow" (Proverbs 13:11).

Most of the readers will probably think that I am going to tell of my dad's work ethic. I could, but I'm not. I am going to let you know about my mama's work ethic. She was the thrifty one in the family; the one that could make a dime go further than anyone I know. She did not have much money or other assets when we were growing up; and she didn't have much when she passed from this life into the arms of the Savior. However, she was the wealthiest person I know. Wealthy....because she had things to show for the things in which she used her money...and her time.

Her wages purchased the necessities of life and the rest went to purchase something for the neighbors, her children, her grandchildren, or the little ones she kept in her home. She would have a gift at Christmas time for everyone. What was her occupation? She ironed for a living while keeping young children of parents that worked. She took in ironing from neighbors, working strangers, and others that did not have time to iron or did not want to iron. She would iron for $.10 a piece, working all day watching the youngsters with an iron in her hand 50% of the time, 20% of the time rounding up kids, and the other 30% cooking meals for the children and neighbors.

I will tell you now that I did not have the same attitude that my mom had with her customers. Most of her customers (ironing and child-care) were very appreciative and supportive of how mom ironed their clothes and took care of their little ones. There were some, however, that caused the end of tongue to be sore about half the time.

What do I mean? Some customers would look at every piece of clothing that mom ironed to see that they were pressed exactly like they wanted them. If a crease was not exactly right they would hand it back to her and say, "When you get it right, you will get your money." Mom would just say that she was sorry and that they could pick up the clothes that did not meet their approval the following day. Mom would have to hold me back from going out the door after them. She would say, "Gerald, my boy, just bite your lip, mumble a prayer under your breath that God would change them, and walk away." Again, my lip stayed sore about 50% of the time.

Of course, Mom had her way in handling ungrateful parents and children. I remember one time when one of the children ran up to her mother when the mother walked in to pick up her little darling, and the child said, "Mommy, I am so hungry. I haven't had anything to eat today." Mom had fed the child a big lunch and a snack about 2 hours before the mom had picked her up. The mother asked mom if that was true. Instead of getting the little girl in trouble, Mom stated, "She might be hungry, but she did get a snack about 2 hours ago." The next day, Mom fed the child at noon, and at 1-hour intervals for the rest of the day. This included a big meal right before her mom knocked at the door. The little girl was so full, she couldn't even talk to her mom that afternoon. The next day, the little girl said, "Mrs. Cumby, has anyone ever died from eating too much?" My mom answered in a way a compassionate, God fearing woman would; she said, "Sweetheart, there probably have been many people die because of eating too much, but I don't think you have to worry."

Since I was not near as compassionate as my mom, I pulled the little girl aside when Mom left the room and told her, "There have been several children die from eating too much....and most of them were 4 years old and had blond hair." You can guess the age of the little girl and what color hair she had.

Yes, I realize that if I was an adult at the time, I would probably be charged with child abuse; but, I was just a 14 year old boy and I enjoyed watching that little girl squirm and curl into a ball for the next 5 hours. Mom made me apologize the next day.

Mother never had a problem with the little girl after that. In fact, the little girl became a big girl and loved Mother like she was her own mother until my mom passed away.

Mom had her way of dealing with anger. She sang or hummed....and mumbled under her breath. She had songs when she was glad, sad, and mad. I don't remember the songs that were sung, but I do remember the difference in pitch of each note. We kids knew when to ask Mom questions and when not to...because the tone and pitch of those special songs gave us hints as to what was going on in her mind.

The seventh paragraph after this one will sound like a grandpa story. You know, one of those, "I walked 5 miles to and from school every morning in snow 34 inches deep." The emphasis, however, should not be on me. The emphasis should be on my mother, the most dedicated self-employed parent I have ever known. She worked from sun-up until 3 hours after sun-down (literally). She gave of her time, her energy, her love, and of her inner self as she worked and prayed for her family. She worked to see that she and her children had the necessities of life.

We didn't have a different set of clothes for each day of the week (but they were always clean and pressed). We didn't have poached eggs, choice of bacon or sausage, orange juice and milk for breakfast every morning (but we had a lot of gravy and biscuits); no chicken fried steak, potatoes, green beans, salad, and a nice dessert for lunch (but we had an egg sandwich or a round-tater sandwich that was filling and satisfying); and, no rib-eye steaks or salmon for dinner (but we did have salmon patties, ground beef steak and green beans and tomatoes from our garden). I never went to bed hungry. I never went to bed wondering if Mom was going to be in the kitchen cooking breakfast the next morning.

We didn't have an alarm clock. We had my mama's built in alarm clock as she woke us up with the rattling of pots and pans in the kitchen. Every morning at 6:00 a.m., our little ears heard bangs and clangs that would wake up the next-door neighbors. She was up-and-att'em getting ready for the day and getting ready to feed us youngsters and all the kids that she would be taking care of that day.

My children today are grown with children of their own. They remember the times we went to see "Nana" (my mama). They remember waking up to mom's alarm clock: the banging of pots and pans. They would roll over in their covers and say, "My gracious, what time is it? Hasn't she gone to bed yet?"

Mom never was late for work. She never did take a leave-of-absence. She never did call in and ask for a day off. She never criticized her boss. She never did complain about her wages. She never talked back to her customers. She loved her job and she was one of the most honest, dedicated persons that I have ever known.

No Japanese or Chinese worker had anything on my mother. It was known (at least in my circles) that Japanese and Chinese workers worked harder and longer than any race during those days in which I grew up. That was true.....with the exception of my mama.

My mom was the symbol of honesty and integrity. She was the greatest of all workers and the best supervisor I know. She supervised herself and she never had to fire or hire anyone. Yet, she was the symbol and shining example of the neighborhood. Her work ethic was impeccable and very imaginative. She kept her checkbook up-to-date and never had to borrow money from someone in the family. She did have credit at Sears and Montgomery Ward. However, Mr. Sears and Mr. Ward never called my mom to tell her she needed to make a payment. She was thrifty, nifty, and spiffy; a great organizer and a great example for kids, newly weds, and "old codgers" to observe and follow her special business techniques.

As a 13-year-old son who had just lost his father, I could not stand for Mom to work so hard to make ends meet. Even though she did not expect me to start to work early in life, I felt I needed to in order to keep Mom from working her self to death. I started working in construction at the age of 13 (summer, 1955); about 3 months after Dad's accident. I have my social security earnings record to prove it. The construction company that I worked for knew that my family needed me to work and make a little extra for our family. I was the oldest of the 3 children at home and the summers were not for me as far as playing summer ball and other extra-curricular activities. I wanted to, but I had to put it out of my mind.

In the summer, I worked in construction from 7:30 a.m. until 5:00 and at the Little League ballpark from 6:00 to about 9:30 as a scorekeeper and groundskeeper. Mother never asked me to chip in for groceries or help with the house payment. She never expected me to give to make ends meet. She was the one that had the bath water ready when I came in at night and a sandwich and a glass of tea before I went to bed. I gave some of my paycheck to help pay for groceries and maybe my little brothers' needs; but it was mainly for my clothes and what I needed for school. Mom was the real provider. She was the one that worried about where the money was coming from to make the next payment. However, she never complained to her children or gave a speech as to how it was up to us to make a few dollars to make the next house payment or pay for the electric bill. She was the light of our home and one of the greatest persons I have ever known.

I didn't realize then, but do now...how much of a liability that the construction companies took when they put me to work before I was 16 years old. If I had been injured, the state and federal government prob-ably would have closed the company down and did it with a substantial fine.

I wish that I could go back now and tell those won-derful people how much I appreciate them for taking a chance with me. They did it for my mom and her fam-ily; but, I did not understand it as a 13 year old.

Chambers Construction, Beck Construction, and E.M. Bailey Bridge Company were my employers from the time I was 13 until I was out of college. They worked with me and they helped my family by giving me the opportunity to learn how to work with dignity and respect. I feel I worked for everything I received as wages. My work ethics were patterned after my mom's. She was a great lady. She lived and died giving hope for the hopeless and a reason to give thanks to a loving God who guides, protects, and takes care of hurting people.

I have to remember, "Life is not about waiting for the storms to pass...it's about learning how to dance in the rain."

"Therefore I tell you, do not worry about your life, what you will eat or drink; or about your body, what you will wear. Is not life more important than food, and the body more important than clothes? Look at the birds of the air; they do not sow or reap or store away in barns, and yet your heavenly Father feeds them. Are you not much more valuable than they?" (Matthew 6:25-26).

Hymn of Full Payment:

Jesus Paid It All

I hear the Savior say, "Thy strength indeed is small!
Child of weakness, watch and pray, Find in Me thine all
    in all."
Lord, now indeed I find Thy power, and Thine alone,
Can change the leper's spots and melt the heart of
    stone.

For nothing good have I whereby Thy grace to claim—
I'll wash my garments white in the blood of Calvary's
    Lamb.
And when before the throne I stand in Him complete,
"Jesus died my soul to save," My lips shall still repeat.

Jesus paid it all, All to Him I owe;
Sin had left a crimson stain—He washed it white as snow.

Text by Elvina M. Hall.

Chapter 15

The Building Of A Patriot

"He who fears the Lord has a secure fortress, and for his children it will be a refuge" (Proverbs 14:26).

"Children's children are a crown to the aged, and parents are the pride of their children" (Proverbs 17:6).

"I will show the holiness of my great name, which has been profaned among the nations, the name you have profaned among them. Then the nations will know that I am the Lord, declares the Sovereign Lord, when I show myself holy through you before their eyes" (Ezekiel 36:23).

My dad and mom were not partial to one of their children over another. What "treats and sweets" one of their children might get on Saturday night as Dad and Mom were picking up groceries at Windham's Grocery in Lawn, Texas, the other children would receive similar "goodies" via the Jumbo Burger or Casey's Restaurant in Abilene.

My dad, after working away from home all week, loved to come home to his children with a bag of goodies with our name on it. The bags contained candy, gum, cookies, and sometimes, games. It was like Christmas every week-end. I wish that I could go back just one more time and tell my dad how much I enjoyed and appreciated the surprises found in those bags. We were "spoiled rotten" and certainly not as appreciative as we should have been.

Of course, my dad's reward for playing "Week-end Santa" was a hug and a "thank you" from each one of us. I think Dad received as much of a thrill as we did as he watched us dig through the sacks and scream with excitement as we opened the little bags of sweet treats that would eventually cause our teeth to rot (the simple pleasures right now do not take into consideration the problems that must be dealt with in the future). Of course, his idea of pleasure and satisfaction was to see the smiles and wonderment on our faces as we bit into a Baby Ruth or Butterfinger candy bar...and maybe even a Holloway sucker that he had picked out "just for us."

A Butterfinger was my favorite candy bar. The employees of General Dynamics and Lockheed Martin know that as a fact; for they received the same type of candy at Christmas time when I was part of that wonderful organization for 38 years. Did you know that Butterfinger candy bars will cause you to have good luck for the rest of the year? Well, it is not so...but it makes for a good story.

Mom was just as thrilled as we were when Dad came home. She might not receive a "goodie bag" from her fellow, but she had the best hug and kiss one could ever get from his treasure chest of goodies.

They were a team, my mom and dad; they loved life and they loved each other. One could not talk about the other without a glow in their eyes and a skip in their step. If that doesn't make a kid happy, nothing will. When they showed their affection in front of us, our hearts were satisfied and gratified.... knowing that everything was alright in the little world of the Cumby's.

I can tell you that the joy expressed by my parents by just looking at each other with eyes aglow and hugging (caressing) one another has been a trait passed on in their children. I, for one, know the real joys of marriage and then passing on to our children the fruition, delights, and treasures that come from "true love."

Even with the above facts in mind, it was true in our home that when my mom was sad, my dad would be sad, also. When my dad was worried, mom was worried. When my mom was happy, Dad would be happy. I know...a perfect partner, from most counselors' thinking and derived consent, is one that balances out the other's attitude or state of mind. In other words, when one is depressed, the other is there to pick them up. This is true in most cases. However, my parents were on the same page; they knew when it was time to worry and they knew when it was time to rejoice. They complemented each other in that both of their minds kicked into gear simultaneously as to what was going on in their off-springs' minds. If one of their children (big kid or little kid) was in trouble or was thinking about getting into trouble, they knew. They would head us off at the pass before we went over the cliff just because "they could sense a storm coming."

Just as they could sense a storm a brewing, they could also sense when we were in danger. It is one of those "instincts" that only parents understand. My parents were the best at this of any parents I know. They knew when Joe was in trouble and they knew when I was in the wrong place with the wrong people at the wrong time.

My oldest brother, Joe (Jody boy, as my granny would call him), was drafted into the Marines at the age of 19. It was at the height of the Korean War (around 1951-'52) and I remember all the fuss that was going on around the house with my mom and dad. When I say, "All the fuss....," I mean some crying and weeping out of fear for their eldest child as they knew where their boy was headed as soon as he completed boot camp.

It was no secret around the homes in America; the Korean War was taking a toll on our troops and our morale at home. Every mother and father with sons 18 to 22 hated to see the mail being placed in the mail box each day. The fear of getting that letter from Uncle Sam stating, "Congratulations, son! Uncle Sam wants you... to report for duty on......" was on every parent's mind. Most of the young men were ready to go and were willing to do their share of giving for their country, but the mom's kept the truth from being heard from their special ones that came from their loins. Sons never liked seeing their mothers weeping and their fathers worrying about their future. However, when the news came for Joe to leave his safe haven of home to go to Camp Pendleton for "boot camp" training, he was ready...but Mom and Dad weren't.

It was a known fact in all of American homes, the Korean conflict was not getting any better....and more and more American kids (soldiers) were coming home severely injured or in body bags. During the Korean War, the United States sent about 480,000 troops to support South Korea in their quest for peace and protection of homeland.

The war began in June, 1950, and ended with an armistice signed in July of 1953. The 3 year war cost our country 33,741 precious loved ones that returned in body bags. There were 92,134 brave young soldiers that came back home wounded; some severely. There were over 4,820 missing in action....never to be heard from again by those weeping mothers and fathers. Of the 7,245 U.S. Prisoners of War (POWs), 2,845 died while being held in a POW camp. Wars are a living hell for those fighting in them and for their loved ones at home patiently and prayerfully waiting to hear that their loved ones were coming home alive.

As much as we have hated to hear of all the young soldiers losing their lives in the Iraq War (approximately 4,300 at this time), there is no equal comparison as to what happened in "the Forgotten War" (Korea).

Don't get me wrong or feel that I am minimizing the Iraq War casualties and wounded soldiers. Every precious son or daughter who has given the ultimate sacrifice for their country is a hero and deserves the highest honor a country can bestow; but, as far as being a war of wars, Iraq did not have near the number of soldiers killed daily, monthly or annually that the Korean War did.

The Iraq War began in March, 2003, and offensive tactics have been suspended since September, 2010.

Where the Iraq offensive by U.S. troops had casualties of an average of 615 per year or 51 per month on the average, the Korean War had over 11,240 plus per year; an average of 912 per month. Now you can see why the moms and dads, brothers and sisters, wives and children were crying themselves to sleep at night as their loved one went off to the "Forgotten War." My parents and siblings were no different. They wailed, and yet gained composure quickly, as they turned this time of their lives over to the Lord.

Joe was really not uptight about his call to service. All of the family was much more concerned than Joe. He was married at the time and the fact that he had to quit his job and start to work for Uncle Sam with a lot less pay was his big concern. He headed off to Camp Pendleton and everyone was sad...and fearful in the Cumby household.

Joe would write and send pictures of accomplishments in his short time in boot camp. Medals for being an expert rifleman and superb marksman were prominent on his Marine uniform when the pictures were sent home. These special marksmanship medals worried my mom and dad. They were proud of his accomplishments, but the talk of him being on a "Special Forces" to go behind the lines of the enemy to do "Special Work" was not a thought that gave Mom or Dad peace about it all.

The scope of Marine rifleman training is that "Every Marine is first and foremost, a rifleman." The manuals go on to say, "To be combat ready, the Marine must be skilled in the techniques and procedures of riflemanship." By the time Joe was out of basic training, he had been indoctrinated and had full confidence in himself as a soldier that would give his life for his buddies and country. He was told that he would get that chance of being on the front lines as he was headed off to the war zone of Korea (I don't remember what they called it. I think the 38th parallel. Forgive me if I'm wrong). He would leave immediately for Korea and he only had a couple of days before he would leave.

Dad came in from work on Friday evening and heard about Joe leaving the next Monday morning. Dad told Norma, Joe's wife, Mom and all of us kids to get ready…. because we were heading to California to see Joe one more time before he left for Korea.

From Abilene, Texas to San Diego, California is an 1177 mile trip and would take about 18 hours to drive it. We piled into our only personal vehicle we had. The vehicle (I don't remember what it was) had no air conditioning and had over 100,000 miles on the odometer. Dad bought one of those whirly bird fans that you put on the outside of the car window as the wind turned the turbines that fanned us. By placing water in the bottom of the reservoir of the fan, we had a little bit of cool air…. at night. In the daytime, the cool water stayed cool for about 30 minutes. Dad became so frustrated with having to stop so many times for fresh water, he finally took the "fang dangle thing" off, rolled down all the windows and headed across the desert through Yuma, Arizona. There was no stopping for motels. We ate hamburgers and baloney sandwiches as we kept tracking and trucking hoping to make it to San Diego by Sunday morning. We made it by Sunday morning with a few hours to spare. Joe was so glad to see us and we were able to converse with him for a few hours before he had to head back to the ship for his assignment in Korea. Joe, of course, wanted to be with his wife for most of those hours that we were in San Diego. As soon as Joe left, we headed back to Texas and were back in Abilene by Wednesday morning. The trip home was quiet and uneventful. Mom sat next to Dad and hugged him most of the way back. It was quiet…with exception to some weeping out loud that you would hear every once in a while. We kids tried to comfort Norma by telling her everything was going to be fine (that's what Mom would always tell us when something was happening that we, under normal circumstance, should fret and worry). I guess we had become accustomed to believing that everything was going to be alright "because my mama said so."

In 1954, Joe came home from his stint in Korea. He was fit and healthy with no injuries. He said that when he arrived in Korea, he was assigned to a unit that needed mechanics to work on the U.S. Combat Aircraft. Because Joe had mechanical skills and had the right attitude, he was assigned as a mechanic working on the aircraft of a well-known pilot during the Korean conflict. The pilot was Ted Williams, the Boston Red Sox, baseball star. Of course, we kids loved to hear the stories about Joe having to put all the parts back on the aircraft when Mr. Williams would come back from a mission.

After Joe settled down from his military duties, he went back to work for Dad as part of the Bridge

Construction crew working for Bailey Bridge Company. The military service probably was the best thing that happened to Joe. He became a true American patriot, loving his country and having a great respect for his dad and mom.

He became a wonderful supervisor of a large work crew working for his daddy. It was only fifteen months after Joe came home that Dad died after the fall from a bridge. When Dad fell, Joe was nearby on a job a few blocks away with a crew working on a culvert on a road going toward Dyess Air Force Base.

What Mom and Dad feared that might happen to Joe, Joe was experiencing now with my Dad's death. Mom and Dad had prayed for Joe's safety while he was at war; and now, Joe was crying out to God that he should have been the one praying for Dad's safety.

Mr. Bailey had so much confidence in my dad and his wisdom and work ethics, that he asked Joe to take my dad's place in management. Joe did that and worked for E.M. Bailey as a Job Superintendent for approximately 28 years. Doyle, Randy, and I all worked for E.M. Bailey at one time or another.

Doyle became a supervisor for Bailey later; and the rest of us kids went on our way to College and worked in our professions with enthusiasm and a desire to always strive for a "Spirit of Excellence" in all we did. Dad and Mom taught us to be a patriot, be a person that loved God, family, and country. Randy, Tony, and I always have respected Joe and Doyle for the many years that they worked hard to make ends meet and to be the best that best can be.

Joe passed away at the age of 66. The testimony at the funeral stated that he had made peace with God through Jesus, his Savior, and that, "chances are that all of those that attended the funeral drove over bridges that Joe and his crew had built as they made their way to the funeral." He, too, was a Bridge Builder.

Thank God for good memories. Those memories are what I dwell on. Like Mom always told us, "If you don't have anything good to say about someone, just don't say it." I had and have good things to say about Joe. He was a good man...and truly a patriot. In fact, all my siblings have strived to live up to the standards taught by my dad and mom. I love every one of them.

Recently, Randy and I were conversing with one another about our times working on the bridges with our brothers (teen-age years). Randy stated, "You know, Gerald, I remember Doyle being one of the best bosses that I have ever had. He would not ever expect you to do something that he would not do. He would help dig a ditch, tie steel, or shovel concrete....even though he was the boss." I believe that is a "hand-me-down" from dad and mom that will stick with us boys as treasures to be passed to our loved ones.

My wife knows that when I speak of my family, my eyes light up and my countenance changes because I know that they want to be a good example for their children and grandchildren. Praise God for life, liberty, and the pursuit of happiness.

"Finally, brothers, good-by. Aim for perfection, listen to my appeal, be of one mind, live in peace. And the God of love and peace will be with you" (2 Corinthians 13:11).

"Whatever you do, work at it with all your heart, as working for the Lord, not for men, since you know that you will receive an inheritance from the Lord Christ you are serving" (Colossians 3:23-24).

Hymn of the Patriot:

My Country, 'Tis of Thee

My country, 'tis of thee, Sweet land of liberty,
Of thee I sing: Land where my fathers died,
Land of the pilgrim's pride, From every mountain side,
    Let freedom ring!

Our fathers' God, to Thee, Author of liberty,
Of thee I sing: Long may our land be bright
With freedom's holy light; Protect us by Thy might,
Great God, our King!

Text by Samuel F. Smith

Chapter 16

To Build Or Not To Build; That Is The Question!

"Suppose one of you wants to build a tower. Will he not first sit down and estimate the cost to see if he has enough money to complete it? For if he lays the foundation and is not able to finish it, everyone who sees it will ridicule him, saying, 'This fellow began to build and was not able to finish'" (Luke 14:28-30).

In his famous work "Hamlet," Shakespeare wrote, "To be or not to be: that is the question:" Another translation with better punctuation would be, "To live or die, that is the question!"

Living or dying? What a choice! Most people would be seriously questioning the individual that would be asking them this question. They would think the person was contemplating suicide, just wanting serious attention, or possibly asking the question of them to "give me the money in your purse, or die. Just make up your mind and I will fulfill your answer to the question."

Yet, Shakespeare is famous for those lines and many people have seriously addressed the quote as to what Shakespeare really meant. The whole speech is tinged with the Christian prohibition of suicide, although it

137

isn't mentioned explicitly. The *dread of something after death* would have been well understood by a more religious-centered audience to mean the fires of Hell.

The speech is a subtle and profound examining of what is more crudely expressed in the phrase *out of the frying pan into the fire.* - in essence 'life is bad, but death might be worse'. For every Christian that understands that there is a hell to shun and heaven to gain, we know that death without the presence of the Lord Jesus in their life, hell is a certainty.

Just as we must face the reality of choosing the right way or the wrong way for our eternal destiny, we must also consider as to whether we are going to build or tear down our lives and others as we journey through this tangled web we call life. "To build or not to build" is a question all of us must come to grips with as we make our choice as to whom we are going to live and share our lives the rest of our days on earth, how we are going to raise our children, and what kind of lives we are going to live in front of our family, friends, and the rest of the world that might be listening and observing as to how we handle life's ups and downs.

To be frank, we can build up or we can tear down; we can give or we can get; we can produce or destroy; we can live life to the fullest or we can check ourselves out before it's our time. My desire is to live life to the fullest; being the best husband, father, grandfather and follower of Jesus Christ as I can be. I plan on taking my final breath in this life praising the Lord....and take the next breath in heaven with the King of Glory, my friend.

While I am riding the "happy trails" in this life, I want to be able to share the joys of laughter, friendship, and the knowledge gained by living. It is one thing to write about it and another to experience and live it. It is easy to put words down on a page as to how one might think life should be. It is another to be able to experience it and to share the drama with others.

As my dad and mom worked through problems, we kids were blessed to share the ride with them. Maybe I was different than most young boys. I certainly did not think I was different at the time, but I realize today, as I have conversed with my brothers and friends of yesteryear, that the details of my home life are like a video that I play back over in my mind time after time. I'm sure that a lot of those experiences as a young boy observing my dad and mom's reaction to life were implanted deep in my sub-conscious mind because they were such an important part of my life. My security hung on their reaction to the "ups and downs" of our world. My world, good or bad, was greatly impacted by what they did and did not do. I was like Linus (Charlie Brown character) and they were my "security blanket."

When I was with my dad on one of his mission trips, I would always hold his hand. In fact, I held Dad's strong hand when he was around from the time I can remember until I was at least 9-10 years old. I felt secure when I was in touch with him.

As far as "one of his mission trips"...let me explain. Dad's mission trips might include a trip to the hospital to visit one of his workers or their family members, a trip to their home to take food when one was ill, or a trip to visit one of his friends or co-workers when they were in trouble and needed a shoulder to cry on. And today, I still feel that those little visits by pastors, deacons, friends and family to those that are hurting are mission trips and are as important as being sent overseas to build a bridge or build a new community church.

Let me tell you about a mission trip in which I went with Dad that will forever be ingrained in my mind... and heart. It was one of those "bridge building" mission trips.

As a boy of about 4-5 years old, I remember one Saturday morning my dad came and took me by the hand and told me that he wanted me to go with him to meet someone. I loved to go with Dad. In fact, if he left and did not take me along, I feared something dreadfully wrong (unless I knew he was leaving for the week to build bridges). You see, I always knew that dad would come back home the next week-end when I would see my mom pack his clothes, wrap her arms around his neck, embrace in a longgggggggg kiss, and Dad would wave good-bye and blow her and us kids a kiss as he was backing out the drive way (if we had a driveway). But on the weekends when he was home, I wanted to be with him.

This mission trip in which Dad had me to go with him involved a trip to Hendrick Memorial Hospital in Abilene, Texas. Upon arriving at the hospital, we went into a room where I heard my dad say, "Hi, Joe, how's my favorite friend today?" I heard the man in bed (of which I could not see at the time) say in a very weak voice, "Mister Jay, I'se doin better today, but I'se still hurting bad." At that time, Dad picked me up high enough to see a black gentleman lying in bed with a tube running from his nose. His big black hand was sticking out from under the cover reaching for my hand and "Joe" said to me, "Well, I'll be, what does we have here, Mr. Jay?" I was reluctant to reach out and take his hand. I had never taken hold of a black man's hand before. Dad quickly said, "Gerald, my boy, shake hands with one of the best men you will ever get to know. Mr. Joe, this is Gerald, my son. Mr. Gerald, this is Joe, my friend."

Shaking hands with Joe was like shaking hands with a large, tough and rough horse's hoof; not because Joe was black, but because his hands were calloused and work ready. Joe was a concrete finisher for Bailey Bridge Company. There is not anything that I know of that hardens and roughens the hands like concrete.

Concrete rubbing/finishing was Joe's occupation. Dad carried Joe on and to the jobs where he was superintendent. He knew that Joe was trustworthy, dependable, loved his family, and was one of the best workers he had found to do the work that needed to be done. Joe honored my dad by giving him his best when he worked on Dad's work project.

I sat in the chair next to dad in that hospital room. I listened somewhat to their conversation. It was about Joe and his condition, about Joe's family, about life, and about God. It was a "memorable moment" for me. Why? I saw a deep concern for each other between these two. Dad knew Joe respected and honored the God that he knew. Joe knew the love and concern Dad had for his welfare, especially Joe's family. As I sat in the chair listening to them and looking at my hand where Joe had squeezed and gently shook, my dad looked over at me and said, "Don't worry, son, the black won't rub off on you." Joe and Dad laughed as I quickly jerked back my hand and placed it in my pocket. A special bond between these two was evident. As I grew older and a little wiser, I realized that my dad and Joe were truly good friends, and were until my daddy's dying day.

There was no prejudiced bone in my dad. However, I grew up in the era when it was common for blacks to ride in the back of the bus; they had their own water fountain and their own area of town where they lived. It wasn't something that I meant to do....expecting the blacks to adhere to society's culture. They call it "prejudiced and discriminatory" today; but, back then, it was just the culture. It was what was natural. I don't know why it was accepted and expected back then, but it was. It didn't make it right, but it was, for sure, the culture.

My mission trip to the hospital ended in a moment I will never forget. I heard Dad ask Joe what he needed in the way of money to take care of his family during those few days in the hospital. Joe responded that his wife had enough potatoes and flour to make bread for his family and the landlord told him he could wait until he could get back on the job before he had to pay his rent; therefore, he didn't know of anything that was outstanding and needed to be paid. I then saw my dad pull out of his billfold two $20 dollar bills and hand to Joe. Joe said, "I can't take that from you, Mr. Jay. You have a family to feed, too." Dad told Joe that he was not asking him to take it; he was giving it to him. Joe, of course, told Dad that he would pay it back just as soon as he could get in a few hours of work. Dad said, "If I expected you to pay me back, Joe, it would not be a gift. Therefore, accept my gift to you and promise me that you will give your wife a hug when she comes up here to your room."

I want you to know, that mission trip with my dad has been deeply embedded into my memory system. Forty dollars in the 1940's would equate to over $500 today.

My dad was making $125 per week when he was killed in 1955. He had just received a raise when he had his accident. So, in the 1940's, that $40 meant about half of Dad's weekly paycheck. It didn't bother Dad to give to Joe. Joe had helped my dad achieve success in life. Joe saw my dad as a friend and a fellow worker. Dad was boss and Joe was willing to do everything to help my dad be successful. At my dad's funeral, Joe was there, crying like a baby because he had lost one of his best friends.

That expression of giving and the faithful friend camaraderie made a lasting impression on my mind to this day. The experience is as vivid now as it was when it happened. By playing that video over and over in my mind and telling my children and grandchildren about that experience has kept the moment alive.

I have never regretted any mission trip I was blessed to go on with my dad. I have spoken at many black and Hispanic co-workers funerals, as well as some of the funerals of their family members in my years on this planet. I cherish our friendship and wonderful fellow-ship over the years. I mention "black" or "Hispanic" friends only to make the reader aware that I don't choose to discriminate; but, because of society's impression that there is some difference between Black America, Hispanic America, and the "White folk", I point out only to identify, certainly not to place one in a different category than another.

We are all Americans, fathers, mothers, sisters and brothers. I know, without a shadow of doubt, that all who have given their heart and soul to the One who gave Himself for the sinner will be together, in one accord, singing praises and shouting glory to the King of Kings…when we cross the Bridge from this life to life everlasting.

"Give, and it will be given to you. A good measure, pressed down, shaken together and running over, will be poured into your lap. For with the measure you use, it will be measured to you" (Luke 6:38).

"A gift opens the way for the giver and ushers him into the presence of the great" (Proverbs 18:16).

Hymn That Reaches the Heart:

Reach Out and Touch..
Reach out and touch a soul that is hungry; Reach out
and touch a spirit in despair; Reach out and touch a
life torn and dirty, A man who is lonely—If you care!

Reach out and touch that neighbor who hates you;
Reach out and touch that stranger who meets you;
Reach out and touch the brother who needs you;
Reach out and let the smile of God touch thro' you.

Reach out and touch a friend who is weary; Reach out
and touch a seeker unaware; Reach out and touch
tho' touching means losing a part of your own self—
If you dare!

Reach out and give your love to the loveless; Reach out
and make a home for the homeless; Reach out and
shed God's light in the darkness; Reach out and let
the smile of God touch thro' you.

Text and Music by Charles F. Brown.

Chapter 17

Building To Build Again

"Now I commit you to God and to the word of His grace, which can build you up and give you an inheritance among all those who are sanctified. I have not coveted anyone's silver or gold or clothing. You yourselves know that these hands of mine have supplied my own needs and the needs of my companions. In everything I did, I showed you that by this kind of hard work we must help the weak, remembering the words the Lord Jesus himself said: 'It is more blessed to give than to receive'" *(Acts 20:32-35).*

There are many other "moments of truth" and "jewels to remember" that I have placed deep in my heart about the Bridge Builders in my family. In this writing, I hope that I have <u>accomplished</u> what I have hoped to <u>establish</u>. What I mean is that I pray that my family, my extended family, my friends, and the readers of this book, realize how important it is to build "beautiful memories as we have the privilege of being blessed and being a blessing to others." <u>If I have accomplished that, then I have established a firm foundation in which others can build on.</u>

It is not good to dwell on the nightmares of the past. It is not good to remind ourselves of the bad situations we have come through in this life; but, it is good to remember and remind ourselves of the way that God has used those situations to make us a better child, parent, sibling, friend or faithful follower of Christ.

Our pastor, Brother Dale Shorter, brought a challenging message recently. It was one of those messages you carry with you to remind yourself to think, pray, and move to action. He based his message on Isaiah 43:18-19, "Forget the former things; do not dwell on the past. See, I am doing a new thing! Now it springs up; do you not perceive it? I am making a way in the desert and streams in the wasteland." That is exactly what I am trying to accomplish and establish. God wants us to look forward....look to the future. Our experiences of the past are just that.... "in the past."

Now don't get me wrong; I love to remember with great detail the things my dad and mom taught me. I know they built that bridge of love and overpass of truth over the troubles and lies Satan has tempted and tried me throughout my days on this earth. Dad and Mom showed me how to walk over that bridge that had already been built for me to get past the dangerous ravines and chasms that waited for me if I made wrong choices. Because of that, it is easier now to recognize the empty holes, dangerous paths, and ungodly traps that Satan has placed on my highway of life.

Thank God, I can pull from my memory how my dad and mom handled situations in life. I am praying that my grandchildren are listening to me and picking out those "moments of truth" as I talk and walk with them in what years I have left to encourage and "hold them by the hand" as they are going through struggles of this life. I pray also that those precious people listening and learning from me as I teach Sunday School and Bible study will be strengthened and established in the truth of the Word in order to meet the challenges of life.

Going back to my pastor's message; he said, **"God is far more interested in our future than our past."** He used 4 points to help the congregation to understand that we need to go on in life in lieu of stopping and looking back. He said:

Stop making excuses

- Don't blame others; understand that nobody ruins your life but you.
- Don't dwell on your failures (have good mentors in your life that rejoice with you when you are successful, and lifts you up when you have failed).

Take inventory of your life; asking the questions: What have I learned in life? What are my assets? Who can help me?

Act in Faith; we tend to get what we expect. We need to focus on the good things.

Refocus on God's Word

- Read through the Bible
- Be careful what you think..."Above all else, guard your heart, for it is the wellspring of life" (Proverbs 4:23).

- Do not rehearse what has happened in the past.
- Trust in God's leading.

I don't think I could have a better sermon or thought to leave with my family, friends, and readers. The sermon goes along with everything that I have said in this writing. I want to be able to listen, learn and leave a legacy for those that want to know the real me.

I don't need accolades or fancy trophies and templates to place on the wall. I just need to know that I have built a few bridges like my dad and mom. I pray that those bridges that I think that I have built are well established and sturdy; and, will be used by many travelers in this life to bring light and a reason to live life to the fullest by all who will or have crossed them. May God get the glory for it all!

"For I am convinced, that neither death nor life, neither angels nor demons, neither the present nor the future, nor any powers, neither height nor depth, nor anything else in all creation, will be able to separate us from the love of God that is in Christ Jesus our Lord" (Romans 8:38-39).

Hymn of Freedom:

Out of my bondage, sorrow and night, Jesus, I come,
    Jesus, I come;
Into thy freedom, gladness and light, Jesus, I come to
    Thee.
Out of my sickness into Thy health, Out of my want and
    into Thy wealth,
Out of my sin and into Thy self, Jesus, I come to Thee.

Out of my shameful failure and loss, Jesus, I come, Jesus,
    I come;
Into the glorious gain of Thy cross, Jesus, I come to
    Thee.
Out of earth's sorrows into Thy balm, Out of life's storms
    and into Thy calm,
Out of distress to jubilant psalm, Jesus, I come to Thee.

Out of unrest and arrogant pride, Jesus, I come, Jesus,
    I come;
Into Thy blessed will to abide, Jesus, I come to Thee.
Out of myself to dwell in Thy love, Out of despair into
    raptures above,
Upward for aye on wings like a dove, Jesus, I come to
    Thee.

Out of the fear and dread of the tomb, Jesus, I come,
Jesus, I come;
Into the joy and light of Thy home, Jesus, I come to
Thee.
Out of the depths of ruin untold, Into the peace of Thy
sheltering fold,
Ever Thy glorious face to behold, Jesus, I come to Thee.

Words by William T. Sleeper.

❦

Chapter 18

And One To Grow On....
The Old Troll Story

"And then the lawless one will be revealed, whom the Lord Jesus will overthrow with the breath of His mouth and destroy by the splendor of His coming" (2 Thessalonians 2:8).

"Since the children have flesh and blood, he too shared in their humanity so that by His death He might destroy him who holds the power of death—that is, the devil" (Hebrews 2:14).

"And the devil, who deceived them, was thrown into the lake of fire, where the beast and the false prophet had been thrown. They will be tormented day and night for ever and ever" (Revelation 20:10).

My favorite story mom used to tell my siblings and I when we were children was about "The Old Troll." I think the true title to the story as it was written was "Three Billy Goat Gruff." Mom just made it easier for us to remember by saying in a gruff voice, "Do you kids want to hear about the old troll again?" I wish that I could tell you that my favorite story growing up was "The Creation Story" or "Jesus dying for my sin"; but I can't; that would be a lie.

Webster's definition of "troll" (noun) is, *"a super-natural creature of Scandinavian folk-lore variously portrayed as a friendly or mischievous dwarf or as a giant, that lives in caves, in the hills, or under bridges."* All I knew as a child was that the "Old Troll" was a bad dude that lived under a bridge that enjoyed eating and tormenting billy goats…..and little kids.

The story of "The Old Troll" or "Three Billy Goat Gruff" (whatever) is summarized as follows:

The story introduces three male goats named Gruff of varying size and age, sometimes identified in the story as the youngster, his father and grandfather, but more often they are described as brothers. There is no grass left for them to eat nearest to where they live, so they must cross a river to get to a better and much more pleasant pasture for food. However, the only way across is over a bridge that is guarded by a fearsome troll who eats any who pass that way. The youngest goat, knowing nothing of this, crosses the bridge and is threatened by the troll but is spared when he tells the troll that his brothers are larger and more gratifying as a feast. The middle aged goat sees that the youngest one has crossed and reaches the conclusion that the bridge must be safe after all; but when he crosses and the troll challenges him, he too tells him of his eldest brother.

When the eldest and largest of them attempts to cross, the troll comes out to seize him but is gored by the eldest goat's horns and knocked into the river. From then on the bridge is safe, and all three goats are able to go to the rich fields around the summer farm in the hills.

Mom always told the story that had the small and middle billy goat gruff to gain access to the other side only by the old troll seeking to make the billy goats a little fatter as they grazed and got a little bit lazier. Then they would have to come back on the other side to their home grazing pasture. When they would cross back over the bridge, then the old troll's intention was to eat the fatter and heavier billy goats. But...the mighty warrior, Big Billy Goat Gruff, was stronger than the Old Troll and won out in the end when he gored the Old Troll and put an end to him.

What a fascinating story in which I see "good and evil" battling it out. Satan being the Old Troll and Jesus Christ being the "Big Brother" or "Grandfather" who challenges and defeats the greatest enemy the world has ever known.

Last week I learned something (Praise God I still have the capacity to learn...something). I was teaching from the Book of Hebrews and while I was studying the Scripture, "Therefore, holy brothers, who share in the heavenly calling, fix your thoughts on Jesus, the apostle and high priest whom we confess" (Hebrews 3:1), I found in a commentary (William Barclay's, The Letter to the Hebrews, page 37), that the Latin term for Priest is *pontifex,* which means a ***bridge-builder.*** The priest is the person who **builds a bridge** between men and women and God.

What a revelation! Jesus is the great high priest (has built that bridge between man and God). Without that bridge to the Father, man would be lost and undone. He or she would never be able to cross over the great chasm fixed between man (because of his sin) and God (who is Holy and righteous). Sin cannot enter into God's righteous heaven, but Jesus has bridged the chasm for us to cross into glory. His death, burial, and resurrection have paved the way for our entrance into glory with Him. He is our Bridge (the creation) and the Bridge-Builder (the One who created the Bridge).

Praise God....The Bridge to God is Toll Free... because the Toll has been paid...in full! The Old Troll won't ever be able to cash in on his plan. He will be defeated by the mighty hand of God.

"But God commendeth his love toward us, in that, while we were yet sinners, Christ died for us" (Romans 5:8).

"For by grace are ye saved through faith; and that not of yourselves: it is the gift of God: Not of works, lest any man should boast" (Ephesians 2:8-9) KJV.

Jesus is the only way to the Father, the only BRIDGE available whereby we must cross into the Promised Land. By trusting the creator (Jesus) of the created (the bridge) we will make it safely across the "great gulf fixed" between man and God, the Father.

Proverbs 6:12-15
A scoundrel and villain, who goes about with a corrupt mouth, who winks with his eye, signals with his feet and motions with

his fingers, who plots evil with deceit in his heart— he always stirs up dissension. Therefore disaster will overtake him in an instant; he will suddenly be destroyed—without remedy.

Isaiah 56:1
This is what the LORD says: "Maintain justice and do what is right, for my salvation is close at hand and my righteousness will soon be revealed."

Ephesians 4:14-16
Then we will no longer be infants, tossed back and forth by the waves, and blown here and there by every wind of teaching and by the cunning and craftiness of men in their deceitful scheming. Instead, speaking the truth in love, we will in all things grow up into him who is the Head, that is, Christ. From him the whole body, joined and held together by every supporting ligament, grows and builds itself up in love, as each part does its work.

1 Peter 2:12
Live such good lives among the pagans that, though they accuse you of doing wrong, they may see your good deeds and glorify God on the day he visits us.

Song…Not a Hymn…But Quite a Story!

I Refuse

Sometimes, I just want to close my eyes and act like everyone's alright..

When I know they're not.

This world needs God, but it's easier to stand and watch.

I could pray a prayer and just move on like nothing's wrong…*But I Refuse!*

I don't want to live like I don't care.

I don't want to say another empty prayer.

Oh, I refuse to sit around and wait for someone else

To do what God has called me to do myself.

I could choose not to move…But I refuse!

I can hear the least of these, crying out so desperately.

And I know we are the hands and feet of You, oh God.

So if You say "move," it's time for me to follow through

And do what I was made to do…and show them who You are.

I don't want to live like I don't care.

I don't want to say another empty prayer.

Oh, I refuse to sit around and wait for someone else

To do what God has called me to do myself.

I could choose not to move, But I refuse!

I refuse to stand and watch the weary and lost cry out for help.

I refuse to turn my back and try and act like all is well.

I refuse to stay unchanged, to wait another day to die to myself.

I refuse to make one more excuse.

I don't want to live like I don't care.

I don't want to say another empty prayer.

Oh, I refuse to sit around and wait for someone else

To do what God has called me to do myself.
I could choose not to move; But I refuse!

Words by Benjamin Glover and Joshua David Wilson

Your Father's Name....Is It Important?

"The most treasured thing you can give a child is a good name."

You got it from your father, 'twas the best he had to give.
And right gladly he bestowed it. It's yours, the while
    you live.
You may lose the watch he gave you and another you
    may claim,
But remember, when you're tempted, to be careful of
    his name.
It was fair the day you got it, and a worthy name to bear,
When he took it from his father, there was no dishonor
    there.
Through the years he proudly wore it, to his father he
    was true,
And that name was clean and spotless when he passed
    it on to you.
Oh, there's much that he has given that he values not
    at all,
He has watched you break your playthings in the days
    when you were small.
You have lost the knife he gave you and you've scattered
    many a game,
But you'll never hurt your father if you're careful with
    his name.
It is yours to wear forever, yours to wear while you live,
Yours, perhaps, some distant morning, another boy to
    give.

And you'll smile as did your father—with a smile that all
    can share,
If a clean name and a good name you are giving him to
    wear.

By Edgar A. Guest.

Quotes for Bridge Building

As a parent, child, or single adult, we can tear down or
build up the confidence we have in ourselves
and the trust we have from others by what
we think, say and do.

The cliché, "actions speak louder than words" is not
always true. What we say can hurt as much,
and sometimes more, as what we do.

We are responsible for our own conduct as others are
listening to and watching us as to how we deal with
problems as well as achievements in life.

We are building bridges in the minds and hearts of
individuals as we make the decisions that will eventually affect ourselves and others for the journey
toward our eternal home.

Acknowledgements

Although *The Bridge Builder* has been written to promote the God embraced morals and character building that I saw in my dad and mom, I feel it necessary that I acknowledge those bridge builders that seldom get recognized for their devotion and dedication to their work and work ethics.

The general public has seldom thought of the bridge builders of America as heroes. They have been taken for granted and by-passed as great American heroes that have made our life easier and safer as we move about in our vehicles on our way to shop, chauffeuring our children to school, and on our way to grandma's house for Christmas. We think about the airline pilots that have flown us to our destination and the responsibility he or she might have on his/her shoulders in making sure that our flight is safe and uneventful. However, the bridge builders all across this great land of ours need to be recognized for their commitment and dedication to the task of building a quality and safe product. They weather rain, sleet, snow and the torrid heat to ensure the bridges are safe and secure for the millions of travelers that move across and under these great structures each year.

Therefore, it is my pleasure and privilege to honor them with this book. As you read this book and see the dedication my dad had for his job and the people that he worked with, you will recognize that he did not do anything great alone. The team of bridge and road construction workers worked together to give us highways and structures that would last and withstand weight and stress over the years. These dedicated workers, whether in management or the ones doing the manual labor, are part of the backbone of America and what America is all about. America works for what America is! The bridge builders promote all the qualities of what America stands for....giving of time, talents, and strength to build a structure that helps fellow Americans get from their home to work and back again, to school and back home again, and to places of play that keep our families involved in keeping our country strong.

So, here is to the bridge builders of America. You are heroes of our time. I would much rather take my hat off to you than any professional sports hero. I wonder if those well-known professional sports heroes of our era would get up at 4:30 a.m. in the morning and work 10-11 hours per day (day after day) for the rest of their lives to make a living for their family?

Thank you, bridge builders, for your dedication and determination to keep the American dream alive! It is the commitment and continued drive to complete "the bridge to some where and every where" that makes you my hero. You are to be commended for this dedication and hard work.

May God give you peace and strength to go on each day. May your days be many and may you cherish every moment with your family. Make every minute count; for you never know what your actions have meant to that little one that is listening and watching as you love and honor your heritage.

Keep up the good work!

The Bridge Builder

By Gerald E. Cumby, a Bridge Builder's Kid

*As you travel across this land of ours and you see the great
historical sights,*
*The wonders of God's creation and go over the mountain
heights;*
*Do you think about the roads and highways that make your
travel possible,.*
*And how these roads make it easier for you as you drive without
a lot of hassle?*

*Do you think about the bridge builders who worked with cal-
loused hands;*
*Who worked in the blazing heat with no air conditioning or
fans?*
Or those who worked up North in the ice, sleet, and snow...
*Do you realize the dedication they must have when off to work
they go?*

*These men and women who get up to go to work before the sun
arises...*
*Come home late in the evening usually to no accolades or sur-
prises.*
*For the routine goes over and over again each day as they try to
make a living.*

*The job is tiring, taking much of their strength, but they just
keep on giving.*

*Do these workers on these bridges get applause and two weeks
off with pay...*
*When they complete the bridge and its dedicated, do the workers
get hoorays?*
*No, they just go to the next project as they get ready for another
day!*
*The idea of showing appreciation for these hard workers...that
is what I pray!*

*The bridge that they are working on has to be finished with no
flaws or it will be rejected..*
*The drivers over these bridges and highways always get what
they have expected.*
*Safe, dependable, and quality work you will get from these pro-
fessional bridge builders.*
*And 50 years from now you will still see the same bridge stand-
ing like great pillars.*

*We take for granted that the bridges are safe and well con-
structed as we travel on vacation.*
*For, as we drive across the many highways that expands this
great and mighty nation,*
*We need to be reminded of the dedication these great American
Bridge Builders have exemplified;*
*For they are what America should be about...giving of ourselves
to help others and in our work take pride.*

Here is to these great Americans...they are truly humble servants that give their best,
To help us get to our destination, back home....and to our place of rest!
We salute you, Bridge Builders! You deserve to be considered for the Hall of Fame.
Even though you might not have received a prize....You have earned it just the same.

Scripture References

The following Scriptures were used or were made reference to in the chapters of this book. These Scriptures will transform your life if you let them. They are the tools used by millions of "Bridge Builders" over the years. Many of these "Bridge Builders" have passed from this life to eternity with their God; but their memory lives on...just like these Scriptures. These Scriptures have been burned, buried, and banished in many countries over the years. However, God's Word will never stop living in the hearts of people. The reason, "God's Word is forever."

Praise God, the Word of God is passed on from one generation to another.

Philippians 4:8	1 Corinthians 3:10
Proverbs 16:3	Proverbs 24:3-4
2 Timothy 4:7-8	Ephesians 6:1
Proverbs 17:6	Proverbs 11:25
Genesis 1:28	Job 19:4
Deuteronomy 6:5-7	Matthew 19:19
Genesis 39:6b-9	Romans 12:1
Proverbs 12:1	Romans 4:7-8
Deuteronomy 6:5	Proverbs 11:24
Proverbs 11:23	Genesis 3:7
Romans 7:24-25a	Hebrews 10:11-12

John 20:29

Romans 6:23

Hebrews 9:27

Joshua 24:15

Romans 8:28

Deuteronomy 6:13

Proverbs 8:13

Numbers 32:23

Proverbs 24:13-14a

Proverbs 3:26

Hebrews 13:7

Genesis 18:19

Psalm 15

Jeremiah 1:4-5

Deuteronomy 10:17

Galatians 3:3

Proverbs 31:28

Psalm 32:7-10

2 Kings 12:15

Matthew 6:25-26

Luke 6:38

Acts 20:32-35

Proverbs 4:23

John 21:25

2 Thessalonians 2:8

Revelation 20:10

Ephesians 2:8-9

Isaiah 56:1

1 Peter 2:12

Romans 3:23

John 14:6

Romans 10:9

2 Samuel 12:21-23

Proverbs 2:6-11

Deuteronomy 31:12

Matthew 5:8-9

Psalm 81:16b

Proverbs 4:1-9

Hebrews 12:7-11

Ephesians 6:1-3

Exodus 18:21

Proverbs 4:23-27

Jeremiah 29:11

Philippians 3:14

Hebrews 6:18

Psalm 32:1-2

Matthew 6:1-4

Proverbs 13:11

Luke 14:28-30

Proverbs 18:16

Isaiah 43:18-19

Romans 8:38-39

Acts 16:31-33

Hebrews 2:14

Romans 5:8

Proverbs 6:12-15

Ephesians 4:14-16

1 Peter 3:16

Bridge Terms—Definitions

Throughout the *Bridge Builder* chapters, I have mentioned various bridge terms/terminology that you might not have understood as one who has never worked on bridges or around bridge construction personnel. There are over 200 distinct bridge terms that can be defined by bridge contractors and structure engineers according to Google and referenced construction and engineering entities. However, I will mention only those bridge terms that I have referenced or need to define to make clear as to how my father lost his life.

Note: My dad fell from a <u>"column cap"</u> (see picture with definition) in which he was checking the concrete to see if forms were ready to be removed after the previous day's concrete pour. He fell from a structure <u>(pier)</u> like the picture with definition. Dad fell only 16' onto an <u>embankment</u> (that would later be completed as <u>rip rap</u>) into a ravine and was there until some of the bridge construction crew working on a <u>culvert</u> approximately 200 yards away noticed his truck smoking from being left running and checked to see about the problem.

1. **Abutment**
    A retaining wall supporting the ends of a bridge or viaduct.

2. **Approach**

   The part of the bridge that carries traffic from the land to the main parts of the bridge.

3. **Brace**

   A structural support or to strengthen and stiffen a structure to resist loads.

4. **Column**

   A vertical, structural element, strong in compression.

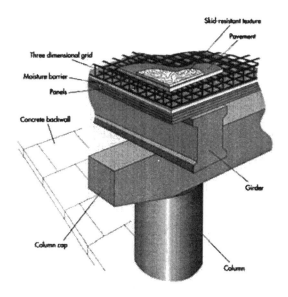

5. **Culvert**

   A drain, pipe or channel that allows water to pass under a road, railroad or embankment.

6. Deck

The roadway portion of a bridge, including shoulders. Most bridge decks are constructed as reinforced concrete slabs, but timber decks are still seen in rural areas and open-grid steel decks are used in some movable bridge designs.

7. Embankment

Angled grading of the ground.

8. Fixed-span Bridge

A bridge without a movable, or draw, span.

9. Footing

The enlarged lower portion of the substructure or foundation that rests directly on the soil, bed-rock or piles; usually below grade and not visible.

10. Forms

Temporary structures or molds made of wood, metal, or plastic used when placing concrete to ensure that it is shaped to its desired final form.

11. Main Beam

A beam supporting the spans and bearing directly onto a column or wall.

12. Pier

A vertical structure that supports the ends of a multi-span superstructure at a location between abutments. Also see column and pile.

13. Pile

A long column driven deep into the ground to form part of a foundation or substructure. Also see column and pier.

14. Pile Driver

A machine that repeatedly drops a heavy weight on top of a pile until the pile reaches solid soil or rock or cannot be pushed down any farther.

15. Rip Rap

Gabions, stones, blocks of concrete or other protective covering material of like nature deposited upon river and stream beds and banks, lake, tidal or other shores to prevent erosion and scour by water flow, wave or other movement.

16. Substructure

The substructure consists of all parts that support the superstructure. The main components are:
- Abutments or end-bents
- Piers or interior bents
- Footings
- Piling

17. Superstructure

The superstructure consists of the components that actually span the obstacle the bridge is intended to cross. It includes:· Bridge deck,
- Structural members
- Parapets, handrails, sidewalk, lighting and drainage features

References: <u>CALTRANS</u> | <u>Caltech</u> | <u>Historic Bridges of Iowa</u>|<u>Indiana DOT</u>|<u>Texas DOT Bridge Design Manual</u>| <u>Washington State DOT Tacoma Narrows Bridge Glossary</u> <u>University of Iowa Libraries Litchtenberger Engineering Library Glossary of Bridge Terminology</u> | <u>Oregon Bridge Delivery Partners</u> | <u>PCI Bridge Design Manual Glossary</u> <u>FHWA Specifications for the National Bridge Inventory</u>

☙☙

"Bridge Building" Terms for the Living

Exemplified by Dad and Mom

1. **<u>Honest, Truthful, Trustworthy</u>**— is frank and open, refraining from lying, stealing, or cheating.
2. **<u>Integrity</u>**— is principled—being of sound moral character, showing courage of convictions, standing up for what is right.
3. **<u>Caring/ Compassionate/ Benevolent</u>**—shows good will, generosity; charitable, considerate, kind.
4. **<u>Courage</u>**—does what is right, even in the face of personal consequences, rejection by others, or danger.
5. **<u>Willing to Sacrifice</u>**—gives of oneself or one's possessions to help others or for something one believes in.
6. **<u>Self-Control</u>**— is able to stay calm and rational, even under conditions of temptation, stress, or aggravated assault (such as being teased or "put down') by others.
7. **<u>Just and Fair</u>**—treats others as you would want them to treat you; rules applied equitably; does not discriminate on improper basis.

8. **Persevering/ Diligent**—puts out best effort and works hard; does not give up easily; keeps trying despite hardships; self-reliant.

9. **Keeps Promises**— attempts to keep commitments, reliable, dependable.

10. **Pursues excellence/ takes pride in work**—does one's best; is not unduly influenced by setbacks or external pressures to do less than one can.

11. **Takes personal responsibility**—is accountable, dependable, amenable; considers consequences and accepts responsibility for own actions or inactions; does not shift blame for own mistakes to others.

12. **Takes Action to Benefit others**—makes decisions that have the potential for a positive effect on others.

13. **Respectful of Others**—acknowledges and honors the rights, freedom, and dignity of others.

14. **Forgiving**—is able to leave upsetting and hurtful things behind; stops the cycle of the hurt to others or oneself; does not seek revenge.

15. **Peacemaker**—is able to compromise, to talk things out without resorting to violence, to seek solutions to problems that will be in everyone's best interests; values calmness and safety. (Oops, dad might have had a problem with this….a little bit!)

16. **Fidelity/Loyalty**—shows faithfulness, trustworthiness; keeps commitments, especially with spouse and family.

17. **<u>Self-respect</u>**—has due regard for one's own reputation and long-term image of a "good" person; does not abuse one's own body or act in trivial ways that are dangerous to oneself; cares about one's own conscience.

All of the above compliments the fruit of the Spirit found in Galatians 5:22-23 (Love, joy, peace, patience, kindness, goodness, faithfulness, gentleness, and self-control).

The Bridge Builder

Volume 1

"And Jesus did many other things as well. If every one of them were written down, I suppose that even the whole world would not have room for the books that would be written" (John 21:25).

Some of the miracles and stories of Jesus were left for the reader as told in His Word. These inspired words and works of Jesus are enough to help us understand who He was and why He came to earth. However, John (in the verse above) lets the reader of the Holy Word know that there are a multitude of stories left unsaid.

With that in mind, let me say that the stories in this book are a few of the many that touched my heart, as well as many others, while my dad and mom walked this earth. Therefore, after this book of memories, there will be another....for the Bridge Builders' affect on my life is

To Be Continued.

A REQUEST:

As you have read the Bridge Builder, it is my desire that the book is not just that….only another book. I want you to realize that it was written to stir something in the reader's heart. Maybe stirring something within you to:

1. **Accept the Lord as Savior if you have not in the past.** Over and over again I have mentioned Scriptures that should have <u>bridged the gap</u> between the person that is without Christ and one that knows where he/she is going after we pass from this life to another. You might have asked yourself what the jailer asked Paul and Silas in the 16th chapter of Acts (New Testament). The jailer asked Paul and Silas "…Sirs, what must I do to be saved? They replied, 'Believe in the Lord Jesus, and you will be saved—you and your household.' Then they (Paul and Silas) spoke the word of the Lord to him and to all the others in his house. At that hour of the night the jailer took them and washed their wounds; then immediately he and all his family were baptized."

2. **Leave an Admirable and Honorable Legacy for your Family.** It is not too late. Whatever your past, today and tomorrow is what counts. Get right with the Lord…and then,

3. **Write it down on paper** where your family can know and understand who you were, what you have done, and how you have overcome heartaches and tragedies to be where you are today.

This is the Challenge...
Now Just Do it!

One of the cherished moments that I will receive from the writing of this book is to learn from the readers as to how it has affected their lives. If you have a story to tell as to how this book either enhanced your life or changed it by pointing to what is the most important part of it....that is, turning your life over to Jesus and learning to become more like the Master, then let me know about it.

Please email me at geraldcumby@att.net and give me your story. God bless you and be sure to:

Give God the Glory for It All!

Meet My Dad and Mom

(Pictures from the Past)

My dad, Floyd Jay Cumby...A handsome man of character and strength. He could pick up a sack of cement with one hand and could, on the other hand, blackout at the sight of his own blood. He could be a strong voice for fairness and, at the same time, be quietly seen as a compassionate man with deep convictions.

Here he is with his "Sunday Go-to-Meeting" clothes on. He dressed up on Saturday evenings and Sunday mornings. Mom said, "There is not a better man in the world than my man." The emphasis was on "my." His life, though short, produced more fruit than many men in the ministry (my opinion). He left a legacy for his children and his children's children by teaching values and character that will stand the test of time. Earth's loss was heaven's gain when Dad breathed his last.

My mom, Edna Glen (Lackey) Cumby, loved life and her children. She loved others as self. There wasn't a selfish bone in her body. She gave when she did not have it to give. Even if it was something she picked up in a garage sale or a "blue light" special at Kmart, she would have that special someone to give it. She would pick flowers or vegetables out of her garden in order to be able to give. She was the most giving person I have ever known.

I have a garden hoe in my possession that she used in her garden the summer of the year she passed away. She was 82 years old and just slipped into heaven to till the ground and tend to the flowers in the garden of God, the Father.

14076087R00122

Made in the USA
Lexington, KY
06 March 2012